Reboot For The Worn Out Professional

by

Steve Corkhill

Copyright Steve Corkhill 2018 all rights reserved

Reboot For The Worn Out Professional

This book is for all those people who are out of sorts for some reason and want to quickly re-energise and regain their life balance.

Everybody gets times when life feels just too hard. You feel tired and weary, worn down by constant demands for your time and attention. It's exhausting. And when you feel like that, your mind filled with clutter and noise, everything seems difficult.

It doesn't take long to spiral into a state where your enjoyment of life and your standards start to slip simply because you are 'too busy'. It can be a lonely and sometimes frightening place. You want your life back. But where do you start?

Well, if you were a computer, you'd hit the reset button and reboot. That clears the rubbish away and re-establishes equilibrium. The same can apply to you.

'Reboot' is a simple three step programme, designed to be applied as a one-off yet one that you will find yourself re-using time and again.

It fits easily into the life of the busy professional because you can dip in and out, selecting and applying techniques as your own circumstances suit. It shows you both *where* to start and *how* to start.

A Reboot is ideal for you if you like:
- To get maximum output with as little input or disruption as possible
- To try fresh ideas that give quick results
- To take an idea and se it as and when it suits you
- To be in control

> *"You may not be responsible for being down, but you must be responsible for getting up."*
> *Jesse Jackson*

Disclaimer

The techniques in this book are based upon research and practice conducted by the author, colleagues and acquaintances. The information contained herein is not intended to replace any existing one-to-one relationships with a qualified health professional. The reader should be aware that this information is not intended as medical advice but rather a sharing of knowledge and information.

The author of this book is not a trained medic, nor is he a professionally qualified personal trainer or nutritionist. This is based on real life experience.
If in any doubt about whether to use any of the suggested techniques, either don't, or simply take the advice of a trained professional and / or your general practitioner before giving them a go. As a professional you are expected to apply common sense about what you are comfortable doing. Neither the author nor the publisher can accept any responsibility for your actions.

If you haven't been active in a while, start slowly and always consult a doctor before starting any program of physical exercise.

Published by FlatBear Publishing
PO Box 3679, Bath, UK. BA2 4WS
First Edition 2015
Second Edition 2018

ISBN 978-1-910291-21-4
www.flatbear.net

The right of Steve Corkhill to be identified as the Author of the Work has been asserted by him in accordance with the Copyright, Designs and Patents Act 1988.

No part of this e-book may be reproduced, stored, introduced into a retrieval system, distributed or transmitted in any form or by any means, including without limitation photocopying, recording, or other electronic or mechanical methods, without the prior written permission of the publisher, except in the case of brief quotations embodied in reviews and certain other non-commercial uses permitted by copyright law. The scanning, uploading, and / or distribution of this document via the Internet or via any other means without the permission of the publisher is illegal and is punishable by law.

Having said that, if you want to pass this book to a few close friends and family, as you would any other paperback, then feel free to do so with my blessings. But please, try to keep it to only a handful, because it really was hard work to produce and copyright laws were developed for a good reason.
Thank you very much for your support.

Reboot For The Worn Out Professional

"There is a battle between two wolves inside us all.

One is Evil – it is anger, jealousy, greed, resentment, inferiority, lies and ego.

The other is Good – it is joy, peace, love, hope, humility, kindness, empathy and truth.

Which wolf wins depends on the one you feed."

Old Cherokee saying.

Table of Contents

Introduction	1
How DO You Get Going Again?	7
How A Reboot Works For You	13
STEP 1 — Power On Self-Test	19
Chapter 1 — Are Your Bits Working?	21
Points To Ponder 1	50
Chapter 2 — The Science of Keeping it Simple	53
Points To Ponder 2	65
STEP 2 — Load Your Operating System	67
Chapter 3 — The Real You	69
Points To Ponder 3	93
STEP 3 — Load Services	95
Chapter 4 — Quick Wins	97
Points To Ponder 4	140
Epilogue	142
Acknowledgements	145
Reading Group Discussion	146
About the Author	147
Also by Steve Corkhill	148
More by Steve Corkhill	150
Connect with Steve	151

Introduction

A few years ago, everything in my life was going well. Little did I know...

I adored my work and had plenty of it. I loved the people and the businesses I was working with and my work / life balance felt spot on. My family were all developing nicely and I was in reasonable physical shape after a lifetime of sport, albeit with a few dodgy joints that grumbled a bit in the winter. I was passionate about continual learning and there was never a dull moment unless I chose it.

As an independent consultant specialising in business projects and the management of change I had the good fortune to work with a wide range of companies in different industries. I was travelling just enough for it to remain fascinating without being exhausting. It included meeting and working with intelligent, motivated people from many nations. Professionalism, enthusiasm and flexibility were my trademarks and I got plenty of positive feedback. I was independent and had a level of income that enabled me to indulge in the occasional luxury. I was enjoying every moment. This wasn't work. Life was pretty good. Did I feel good? You bet I did! This was wonderful.

Then things slowly began to change...and I allowed them to change. My error.

I began taking little things for granted. I got too comfortable. Staying in contact with people became a chore rather than a hobby. I allowed my physical activity to drop off and the quality of my fuel in all forms to plummet. So I began to look and feel untidy, tired and out of balance. My focus on development and growth slipped away to be replaced by the poison of routine. I found myself saying "I used to..." with disturbing frequency. My enthusiasm and energy ebbed away, avoidable errors crept in and slowly the enjoyment escaped. I had stopped moving forwards and the fun had gone.

And even though I was aware of all this happening, I didn't do much to arrest it because I was too comfortable. Frankly, I had become complacent.

One day, one of my contracts wasn't renewed. Shortly after, another was cancelled. Soon I noticed that younger people were being given the roles on some projects where once I would have been the unquestioned number one choice. I felt flattened and demotivated. Gradually the phone stopped ringing. Then I got scared as well.

That was the turning point. My comfort zone had become too comfortable. Action was needed. But what?

I was demotivated, scared and worn out. Where on earth should I start?

I began to look around and found a huge number of programmes that seemed to fit the bill. However, they all demanded that I make radical changes to my whole life, to commit absolutely to rigid pathways or to realign my whole being to focus on a long term goal. Nah. That didn't suit me.

I wanted something to get me quickly back on track. Some short and sharp ideas that I could use immediately and easily incorporate into my life. I already had an established set of goals to dust down, so I was happy with what to do once I had found my spark again.

The problem was getting started again. I needed a short, targeted project with the specific aim of providing me with a set of energising tools to rebuild my confidence, energy and fire.

And so the idea of a personal reboot came about.

> A reboot. Not a life review, simply an efficient kick-start to get things working again. And I wanted to KISS it ('Keep It Simple, Stupid') because long experience has shown that complex solutions don't work without a LOT of effort.

I took action. I began with ten of the Quick Wins in Chapter 4 and at the same time started to research the idea, because I wanted something that was both pragmatic and different from the standard fare in the self-help books.

I dug into notes and books from the many courses I had delivered and attended over the years. I delved through libraries of self-development books, spent hours discussing with specialists and scoured the Internet for novel ideas. I noted advice from friends and colleagues with hundreds of cumulative years of experience between them and recalled lessons from my own work as a coach, trainer and lifelong student of development. Any ideas and techniques needed to be fun as well as effective.

Inevitably, I wandered off along many tangents and disappeared down a number of rabbit holes (crikey, there are some mad ideas out there!), but gradually I whittled them down to the best strategies and practices, trying them all out along the way.

The more I discussed the idea with colleagues and friends, the more they said that they could relate to the idea. Everyone has encountered worn down periods in their life. They could all use a set of proven, quick-acting pick-me-up ideas to call upon when needed.

"Why don't you put them all into a book?" they said.

"Because I'm not exactly J.K. Rowling or William Shakespeare," I said.

"Just do it" they said.

From there the idea of *'Reboot for The Worn Out Professional'* was born – a collection of techniques with a structure, using a computer reboot as the analogy.

Some of the seven techniques are truly simple, some are quite sophisticated and many have multiple uses. Pick and mix the ones that work for you. They are all tried and tested and they have worked successfully for me and many others too.

Suffice to say that you will be free from any nagging or fixed approach here. You are a professional and the decisions are yours about how you incorporate these ideas into your life. Above all, have fun!

Steve

'Reboot: Pronunciation: /ri:'bu:t
VERB, NOUN
Restart or revive; give fresh impetus to."
[Oxford English Dictionary (OED)]

"Worn out: Pronunciation: /w Pr aaP
ADJECTIVE
Extremely tired; exhausted, fatigued." [OED]

"Professional: Pronunciation: :/prr/pru(rr/prunci
ADJECTIVE, NOUN
A person who is expert in their work." [OED]
...and who has a great basic attitude.
[My qualification]

How DO You Get Going Again?

How do you get excited again after you've been doing something for years? How do you get back to feeling that buzz and enthusiasm about everyday things around you?

Reboot, that's how.

A reboot plays to all your strengths as a professional without causing you extra work or making unwanted demands on your time. And it's pretty much free. None of the exercises in this book require any financial outlay. The only necessary cost is some time.

It is a quick and effective way to get better results rapidly for relatively little effort. And, as the key element is to have a bit of fun and play along the way, whatever effort you put in will be enjoyable.

Who is this for?

"Professional: One who is expert in their work."
[Oxford English Dictionary]

I use a broader qualification of 'professional' than the OED's definition above. I strongly believe that you can be a professional in any walk of life.

The 'professional' comes with a few basic expectations on top of the presumption that you are 'expert' or 'very good' in your work:

- You always try to improve and learn
- You are happy to try new ideas
- You are a nice person who enjoys work, life and other people's success.

  Either male or female, of course. It is intended to be enjoyed by both men and women and every idea is applicable to both sexes. If I use the word 'he' in the text, please read it as relevant to both. Or all, as the case is becoming.

Obviously, you're also bright, keen, instinctively willing to help and don't rely on being a passenger or political correctness to get by. You accept that life is sometimes unfair and throws up unexpected problems. You treat them like bumps in the road to get over. You take responsibility for yourself because 'professional' is more than a job title. It's also a state of mind and action…. and most certainly not about being self-centred. Focused – yes; self-centred – absolutely not.

Not everyone meets the definition

Take these examples – names obviously changed to protect the innocent. i.e. Me.

I met a bloke at an international rugby match who held a senior position in a global organisation. He fitted the definition of a professional perfectly except for one thing: he was a complete and utter arse. He was so full of his own self-importance and negative opinions of anything other than himself that it poisoned the atmosphere and enjoyment for everyone around him. This book is not for the likes of him.

Then there is the high achieving rampant feminist who aggressively pushes and stretches the career boundaries for women in a challenging and occasionally hostile environment. A wonderful role model until the day he started to believe his own hype and everything became all about 'I' and 'me'. It became "My way or the highway", with alternative viewpoints treated with contempt and ignored. This is not for him.

On the other hand, I was in a pub when I first encountered the guy who had left school early with no qualifications. He was loud, as drunk as a Lord and he stank of sweat. Yet he has this fantastic reputation as a master builder and stonemason. His work is so consistently excellent and he has such a terrific manner with people that he always has a long waiting list of business throughout even the hardest recessions. He belongs in the 'Professional' book.

My pals Mark and Seamus somehow bring a sparkle to Project Office and Financial Accounting work (honestly, they do. Even David Blaine hasn't achieved THAT yet!); Amanda leads sales teams with extraordinary style and Karen demonstrates a mastery of child minding, controlling and guiding every one of the overprotected little sods that come her way with a saintly calm and a confident smile. All qualify because of their manner and attitude. They are the type of person this book is for.

'Professional' isn't about qualifications, or whether you work in a field that is regulated or has historically been granted the status.

It isn't limited to a good level of income, either. Kevin pulls in over $15 million in a bad year and Peter lives on a stipend of about $5,000 a year. Both belong.

Being a professional is about your manner, your mindset and the way you treat and support people.

⏻

So you qualify as a professional? And you're still with me? Excellent.

Of course, while there are a lot of upsides to being a professional, there are also some downsides.

Excellent preparation, self-control, good judgement and polite behaviour are all expected as standard. Like the Boy Scouts or Girl Guides, you need to "be prepared at all times".

Many of these eternal expectations will be contributing to the way you felt when this book first caught your attention. If you've got this far then frankly you're no longer browsing nonchalantly. You have a problem that needs fixing and you're interested in discovering more about your personal reboot.

Meeting these expectations of 'being a professional' is demanding, draining and sometimes you really don't feel like playing the game when you're tired, worn down or lonely. Especially if that 'sometimes' seems to be coming around more often.

Time was when your energy seemed to galvanise and enthuse the people around you. Your ideas were so on fire they positively crackled. Recently though, you may feel you've only been firing on two cylinders for a whole bagful of good reasons. It's no fun to feel worn out and drained, especially when you used to have such energy or when everyone else appears to be enthusiastic relative to you.

Oh, that damned phrase 'used to'. How many times do you say it and cringe a little bit inside or think wistfully of times gone by?

The bottom line is that 'it' ain't working, so you know you need to do something about 'it'. With all your experience you'll know but are perhaps more reluctant to accept that the only way to stop feeling this way is to DO something differently. To get your fire back something needs to change, and you are the one who can make that happen. The good news is that I and millions of others are testimony that you can!

Hit that reset button and start your reboot.

"Reboot; Restart or revive; give fresh impetus to."
[Oxford English Dictionary]

When a computer is rebooted it goes through a basic three step process to restore it to as close to 'as new' as possible after the power has been reconnected:

- It checks that all of its bits and pieces are working: the memory, the power unit and the peripherals. This is known as the 'Power On Self-Test'
- It reloads its operating system – the core rules that govern the way it works
- Next it loads special mini programmes called 'Services' that run in the background to help it to run more efficiently

At the same time all the trash that has accumulated in its memory is erased. Soon the reboot is completed and the system awaits the first user input.

   A reboot fires up the computer and it will fire you up, too. It's a new beginning.

   What will you do next?

How a Reboot works for you

Your reboot is laced with principles taken from the 'Five Ways to Wellbeing' – the simple, yet highly effective concepts of Move, Connect, Give, Learn and Notice. Employed together with enthusiasm and willingness they help you move smoothly on from your worn out state to feeling energised and enthusiastic again.

The Five Ways are from the New Economics Foundation. In 2008, a UK-based think tank identified a set of evidence based actions to promote and develop wellbeing. Those five are to 'Be active', 'Take Notice', 'Connect', 'Keep Learning' and 'Give'. They may be well over ten years old, yet they are still highly relevant.

Each person is an individual so you won't find any prescriptive rules in this book. Use it to fit with yourself.

Step 1 establishes your baseline. In the computer analogy, this is the 'Power On Self-Test'.

Step 2 draws out what influences and drives you. Or reloads your 'Operating System'.

Step 3 loads up a toolkit of quick and effective 'Services' to help you run yourself efficiently.

*"If you don't know where to start, make a choice of doing a single small thing from one of these actions:
move, connect, give, learn, notice.
In the short term, concentrate on the first two, which mean remembering that you're a physical and social animal"*
Psychologies Magazine

Little things, big impact

Even the smallest changes can have a big impact. That's a big factor in your reboot.

In a paper for the New York Academy of Sciences in 1963 an MIT meteorologist called Edward Lorenz posed another unnamed meteorologist's suggestion that, if the mathematical chaos theory was correct, a single flap of a single seagull's wings would be enough to change the course of all weather systems on earth.

Lorenz was developing a computer programme to determine the likely development of weather systems based on current conditions. One day he was entering data and missed out the last three of six decimal places on one of the numbers, leaving a difference of a few millionths of a digit from the original value. When the new number was used he found that the very small change had produced a major swing in the results. It was an interesting and significant observation.

Alas, as with all great concepts it was immediately met with a harrumph, was ignored and everyone got on with swinging through the Sixties, building big space rockets and listening to The Beatles or, for the more rebellious, The Stones or The Who.

In a 1972 talk to the American Association for the Advancement of Science, Lorenz used a more poetic phrase when he posed the rhetorical question "Does the flap of a butterfly's wings in Brazil set off a tornado in Texas?" That got more reaction and a legend was born.

The Butterfly Effect' is now a metaphor for any situation where a small change can have huge impact. Like an enormous avalanche can be triggered by a gust of wind or small noise, or how a fragile O-ring could change the path of space travel for decades.

In 1986, the Challenger space shuttle blew up 73 seconds after launch. The unusually cold weather had caused a failure in a simple O-ring that resulted in a massive explosion. That single blast changed the whole perception of space exploration and accelerated the end of the Shuttle programme. As it was, the whole programme was halted for three years. It delayed planned launches of many satellites and deeper space programmes didn't start again until the 'Orion' programme was started with a trial launch at the end of 2014. All because of a fragile O-ring – a small change having an enormous impact. Most of us have direct experience of this: just think how big an impact it has when you break a thumb or a little toe, get a paper cut or toothache. Flexibility and balance fly out of the window. Inconvenience escalates out of all proportion.

When you make relatively small changes to your circumstances, the knock-on effects can be spectacular. It's an important principle for your reboot.

Step 3 introduces thirty two tried and tested, quick acting techniques you can use to inject and rebuild your fizz, enthusiasm and energy. The majority use your existing skills and can be easily fitted into your life.

Some effects are subtle yet hugely significant – such as the impact that simply standing tall and smiling has on others around you, let alone the emotional, physical and motivational impact it has on you.

The main aim of the reboot is to enable you to emerge enthused, energised and excited once again.

It utilises three important tenets:

- You can change your physiology by changing your mind and you can change your mind by changing your physiology
- What goes around, comes around. Your efforts are reflected back to you in how the world responds
- You can get even greater results when you look beyond yourself and focus efforts on other people.

As an example of how your mind can affect your physiology, try this little exercise:

Briton James Kingston is a character who loves to climb the tallest and highest cranes then hang off them with one hand and no support. Close your eyes and imagine you are standing next to him on his next adventure. You are at the top of the tallest crane on top of the tallest building, looking down past your toes at the tiny people and cars driving far below. Feel the wind buffeting you and remember that the strut you are standing on is only two inches or five centimetres wide.

Now – what's happening to your heartbeat? Most people experience a slight increase in heart rate and sometimes a little breathlessness when they think about this situation. Yet they haven't moved. This is an example of your mind affecting your physiology.

Any change requires action on your part. You can outsource some things but you can't outsource the learning, the thinking and the growth.

"If you want to change anything, all you have to do is either start behaving positively or stop acting negatively."
Unknown

So let's kick off Step 1 – the 'Power On Self-Test'.

STEP 1 – Power On Self-Test

As soon as your computer is turned on, the basic input-output system (BIOS) on the read-only memory (ROM) chip is 'woken up' and takes charge. BIOS first does a 'Power On Self-Test' (POST) to make sure all the computer's important components are operational.

OR: How are your bits?

Chapter 1 – Are your bits working?

"Hey – how you doin'?"
Joey, Friends

Your 'Power On Self-Test' is about establishing a baseline and checking your bits. Remember that the focus is on flexibility, balance and fuel from a physical AND mental perspective.

When you know your starting points in terms of these reboot basics, you can measure your progress at any point of your choosing.

As a professional, the concept of planning should be very familiar: work out where you are and where you want to be, put together a set of steps to get there with the available resources and then put it into action. Check along the way that things are working as expected adjust as required. Everything then goes nice and smoothly, doesn't it?

So — how are you doin'? This, the very first step in your reboot, involves finding out. You shouldn't be surprised to discover that it includes some moving, connecting, giving, learning and noticing, some optional light physical effort and a bit of thinking.

The intention is for you to have fun along the way.

Fun means it is to be enjoyed. Permit yourself to be

a child again, revel in the experiences and don't get tied up by theory.

In 2006 when my wife Betsan was setting up Stitchlinks.com, a health-based website, she was challenged by academics and clinicians about how she could claim that knitting was an effective tool for improving wellbeing. She listed over twenty very powerful reasons from her research at the time and cited the many hundreds of testimonials she had been sent from around the world. Then she made the error of saying that "It can also be fun!"

Fun? Fun?? FUN???! One senior clinician in particular was beside himself. She received a full dressing down by email about how the concept of fun — full definitions included — was not in harmony with the exigencies of the double-blind research testing methodologies required to support any hypotheses as it is immeasurable for said purposes and as such must be permanently excluded from any considerations. Oh, for goodness' sake.

What's your status right now? Yep, you're feeling worn out. But what else?

On the subject of status checks, it is a good idea to visit your doctor. It just may be that there is something else that is causing your worn out feelings. The good doctor will also be able to tell you if you are fit enough to do any of the suggested physical challenges. (If he proposes giving you drugs to boost your mood, question it).

OK, now that necessary warning is out of the way. From now on you are presumed to have common sense and to take everything in this book as guidance only. Make your own decisions in consideration of your personal circumstances. Have fun – it might be the only catalyst you need to start firing on all cylinders again.

Baseline

You need to know where you are now before you can get to where you want to be. Step 1 is about establishing a baseline so you can notice your reboot working and having an effect.

The activities focus on your most useful assets as a professional – your flexibility, your mind and your connection with other people.

It is natural for human beings to seek to improve and thrive on success. Success breeds success and it gives us a buzz. "No shit, Sherlock" as my mate Sean would say. But yes, it does, and that thought is one I suggest you keep at the front of your mind during this reboot. It's based on the simple truth that we attract more of what we think about. Think about success and guess what? You will start to notice your own successes. Even better, you may recall from your own experience that true success is made up of a lot of small successes rather than a couple of big breaks.

The first time you play with any of the suggested activities in this chapter you may be surprised at what emerges. Accept it, remember it, and then try again when it suits you. There will be at least two of them that you repeat immediately...

Your results won't be perfect. Indeed, if they are then you really don't need this book. Try each activity to establish which bits are working and which may need working on.

You will start to feel better as your mind moves back to anticipating positive results. Each activity has been selected because it gives big results for small effort, which could of course make you feel just a bit smug. Enjoy the sensation.

There are fourteen activities in this chapter, each of which can be completed in a matter of minutes and often even seconds. The results are yours to use for your own benefit and benchmarking. Share them with a close friend if you wish, although that is not a requirement for your reboot to be effective.

Do them at any time, just about anywhere. Have fun doing them alone or perhaps try introducing some of them as icebreakers in meetings and in workshops because they work splendidly in those contexts too.

Keep a log

Some people like to keep a log of the reboot. It enables them to make comparisons later. Take a note of any measurements you make the first time round, so you have a base to compare with when you decide to repeat them at a later stage.

There is no end time to a reboot. Go at your own pace, work with what suits you and try the techniques with an open mind. You may be surprised at how quickly it works.

If you do decide to keep a log, score yourself out of 10 for each activity. It is subjective, relative and unique to you so there's no need to beat yourself up over any thoughts of comparison with others.

OK. Let's go.

Stand on one leg, eyes closed. Touch nothing

Your target is to stand for 30 seconds on each foot. No peeping or cheating. You don't really need a watch. Simply counting out the seconds will work fine.

This test is used clinically to identify your physiological age, which may well not be your actual age. If you managed to do 30 seconds easily you will be either very young or a highly impressive person.

The average time for a 60-69 year old is 10.2 seconds (yes, 10.2), for a 50-59 year old about 21.0 seconds and for anyone below 50 it is just over 24 seconds.

How did you do? This is a great way to test your balance and concentration.

You can improve your time noticeably with regular practice — just 30 seconds each leg — and do yourself a whole lot of good at the same time. As you improve, knock back those years and actually become 'younger' with practice!

Every practice improves your balance and posture. It will make you laugh as you windmill around out of control for a second or two and help to strengthen your 'second heart' in your calf and lower leg muscles. Incidentally, this is a great party trick and gets immediate attention as it is so simple.

Your 'second heart' is the system of muscles, veins

and valves in your foot and calf that pump blood back up to the heart and lungs. When they become weak, blood can pool and cause swollen ankles, varicose veins, spider veins or even blood clots. This system works hard in order to fight against gravity, so it makes sense to work on it.

Note your time for each leg. If you like a challenge, you'll enjoy the buzz you get each time you beat your record. Remember — success breeds success so will build your confidence and general feel-good factor.

Kneel down and sit back on your heels

It's as simple as that. Sit on your heels. Kids can do it easily. Less easy for adults after a while.

This is another great check of physical flexibility. Many people struggle with this if they have been relatively inactive over the years. Sitting for long periods in particular can result in stiffness in your back, hips and knees. Give it a go. It will get easier with time.

Give yourself a score out of 10 for how well you did.

When you sit on your heels it stretches your thigh muscles and reduces the pull on the knee when you're standing, as well as helping your hip and lower back muscles to support you more easily. That means it can prevent lower back pain, which is a Good Thing.

Our Physio reviewer pointed out that sitting on your heels also requires flexibility in the knees, hips and lower back, so some additional gentle stretching may be required to help the exercise.

Achieving my first 10 score after living with ever stiffening limbs for a long time was one of my most satisfying personal achievements in years.

Sitting on my heels had been impossible for a long time until I put in a little effort to stretch and strengthen the muscles around my knee, hips and back. You really notice the extra flexibility in everything you do. It's significantly less painful, for a start.

Gradually I improved and finally managed to do it with a huge smile on my face. What a buzz. It's not much when you write it down, but that became one of the my most satisfying physical achievements in over a decade. Very pleasing.

Make pictures in your mind

Concentrate. It may help if you close your eyes.

- Describe the front door to your home. What does it look like? What colour is it? Is there any furniture on it, like a knocker or a keyhole? Where is it on the door? Some will find this easier than others.
- Picture yourself opening it. Which side is the handle? Does it open inwards or outwards? Open at the left or the right? Is it wide or narrow? Is there a threshold or a step? Step inside. What do you see immediately?
- Now change the image. Imagine you are watching yourself approaching and then opening the door. Can you see yourself? What do you look like?

If you can do this exercise, it is a start in helping you to harness and use some of the extraordinary power of your mind, your single greatest asset. If you can't, take a good look at your front door next time you are there, then practise and practise more. By working on controlling the pictures in your mind you will develop a crucial skill.

Give yourself a score out of 10 for how vividly and accurately you managed it.

Being able to construct a scene in your mind means you will be able to benefit from visualisation techniques in the future. These are increasingly used to great effect both clinically and in training the likes of elite athletes and managers to improve their performance and enjoyment in all areas. In fact, the majority of professional sportsmen and most professional presenters and speakers use visualisation to give them confidence to perform in front of large crowds. Indeed, successful and elite sportspeople often talk about their success being "10% effort, 90% mental".

When you can switch the scene from one where you are looking out of yourself to one where you are seeing yourself as if in a movie, you can begin to 'associate' and 'disassociate' your thoughts.

This is a remarkably powerful ability to develop as it will ultimately give you control over your thoughts and feelings at will. Now THAT is an incredible thought.

What's your vibe?

- What is your vibe like nowadays? Are you helpful? Constructive? Cheerful?
- Would you want to spend a lot of time with you? Others will feel your vibe so it matters.

Your attitude affects everything you do – how you connect, how you learn, who you notice, how or whether you 'give' and even how you hold yourself or move. More significantly, you may or may not know that it affects everybody you meet.

What goes around comes around. It's true. In general, others will be sensitive to your vibe and will reflect your manner and attitude back to you. Give out crap and you'll get it back; give out positivity or encouragement and they will come back to you by the truckload. Your vibe and how you demonstrate it influences your whole living and working environment.

And your attitude is something over which you have sole control. Nobody else can determine your attitude in any circumstances, ever.

Many people who are deemed to be 'successful' tend to have a positive nature and outlook because they understand the impact it has on others around them. As a general rule people enjoy being with those who have a positive attitude as they radiate cheerful and constructive energies. Everybody picks up on the vibes you give off unconsciously, even when you may not be aware of them.

You communicate with everybody at all times through every part of your being. You start to influence people a long time before they hear your first words. It's very difficult to hide your attitude.

So – how is your attitude in relation to what you would consider ideal?

Give your vibe a score out of 10. Be honest.

How do you do?

Or, more directly, how well do you get on with people?
- This is one to look at yourself in the mirror and ask your true thoughts.
- There's no need to go out and survey the general opinion; you already know in your heart of hearts. The more honest you can be with yourself, the more powerful your reboot will be.

As a professional you will have many connections with others. Everything that an individual can buy or produce is the result of a coordinated effort from a lot of people. Nobody can be successful without the efforts of others, so it makes sense to get on with them.

In his famous book 'How to Win Friends and Influence People', Dale Carnegie believed that financial success is 15% down to professional knowledge and 85% to "the ability to express ideas, to assume leadership and to arouse enthusiasm among people".

First published in 1937, over 15 million sales and more than 80 years later this book is still in demand, regularly appearing in Amazon's best sellers.

You may not have time to read it, so here's a summary in eleven words:

Avoid arguments; Show respect; Be friendly;
Do not overpower; Be nice'.

It always strikes me that there is a certain consistency in this advice, regardless of decade or where you are in the world. All of these supposedly old fashioned values are as true today as they were when it was first written. And they are all able to help your reboot as you look out towards other people.

Even in our modern, technology-driven culture, the ability to get on with people is one of the single most useful skills you can work on. It is a really simple truism — people like people who are nice to them.

So how well do you try to get on with other people? Honestly? Give yourself an honest score out of 10 for how well you believe you do it.

Do you help others?

> *"There are two ways to exert strength.*
> *One is pushing down; the other is pulling up".*
> Booker T. Washington, Civil Rights leader

Helping people involves connecting, noticing, giving and receiving. It develops your psychological flexibility and provides invaluable social and emotional fuel leading to balance in life.

A basic principle of most democratic societies is that people treat others the way they would like to be treated. Helping is both nice and the right thing to do.

Helping other people makes you feel good. It takes you away from selfish, self-centred thoughts and leaves you feeling strong inside.

Helping people also triggers the powerful principle of Reciprocity. This states that if you help somebody, they usually feel a debt and often return something of a greater value.

Reciprocity is the first of Robert Caldini's six principles of influence described in his 1984 book '*Influence: The Psychology of Persuasion*'. The good cop / bad cop strategy is a good example of the principle. If anything is predictable in human behaviour, it's the principle of Reciprocity. It is worth noting that it works the other way, too: do bad things and people remember them.

The six principles are sometimes also known as the

six *weapons* of influence because of the way they are occasionally misused to influence or persuade. The six principles are Reciprocity, Commitment, Social Proof, Liking, Authority and Scarcity.

It is a fascinating book to study separately, away from your reboot.

Helping people is good on every level. For your reboot, it will be an energising and constructive challenge to be the one to help people up, to raise their ambitions and hopes in a small way. It's quite a challenge to undertake as, other than making you feel good about yourself immediately, any other returns may take a bit longer.

How much do you help people in relation to what you would consider ideal? Score yourself out of 10.

Do you practice being 'in the moment'?

Try this short exercise:
- Take yourself away for 2-3 minutes to breathe
- Close your eyes and concentrate completely and solely on your breathing
- Feel when you breathe in, then feel it again as you breathe slowly out
- Try to make your concentration total. Be aware of the moment, and everything happening within it
- Notice sounds or sensations around you, allow yourself to become aware of any movements
- Concentrate on being aware without making any judgmental thoughts.

Being 'in the moment' is a powerful skill for your mental balance and flexibility.

It is impossible to worry when you are truly 'in the moment' because all worry is either about the past or the future. Being 'in the moment' involves being fully aware of NOW, not allowing concerns of the past or worries about the future to invade.

If practised frequently it will provide a foundation for later investigations into meditation and mindfulness along with all of the benefits that can come from them. In recent years many magazines have picked up and confused the oncepts of mindfulness and meditation.

The two are not the same. Being able to concentrate so hard that you can be 'in the moment' is, however, a very useful skill that will come in useful if and when you want to investigate them.

Were you able to engage fully in being 'in the moment' or did you find yourself worrying about work or your 'to do' list?

Give yourself a mark out of 10 for how well you consider you did. It's not easy.

Do you 'switch off'?

How often do you 'switch off'? Have you got a regular, relaxing past-time that helps you to do so? Do you 'switch off' for a little bit every day?

In our 24/7 world it can be difficult to take a break from the deluge of external influences such as social media and emails. Many people may never switch off.

'Switching off' on a regular basis is essential for health and it can so easily just fall by the wayside in busy professional lives. Instead we accept the ongoing pressure and demands of our jobs and the stress that slowly builds up in our minds and bodies. Not switching off regularly is detrimental to wellbeing and may well have contributed significantly to your worn out state.

'Switching off' helps you to feel calm, relaxed, unflustered and in control. It will help to disperse those stress hormones building up in your system.

Activities you enjoy, such as engrossing hobbies and sports, will enable you to switch off. As you become absorbed in an activity you will enter a wonderful state of 'flow' – an optimal mental state described as being "carried away by a current, effortlessly like in a flow".

> *"We are at our happiest when we are in a state of oneness with an activity. As we engage in our favourite tasks we get 'in the zone' – in a state of 'flow' and become unaware of the passage of time."* Mihaly Csikszentmihalyi

When time is tight, try taking a short walk to give your brain a break or sing your heart out in the shower to an imagined audience. If you can engage fully and completely ithen you will be 'switching off'.

Incidentally, watching TV isn't a recommended activity for 'switching off'.

Score yourself out of 10. It's a big fat zero on this one if your mind is constantly on the go 24/7.

Once again, simply working on this may be all you need to reboot and get yourself back on track.

How often do you really stand tall?

Try this exercise to stand tall:
- Stand as if there is a golden thread pulling the top of your head gently upwards
- Gently elongate your neck and your spine
- Tuck your chin in a little
- Roll your shoulders back and ease your shoulder blades down
- Gently tighten or brace your stomach muscles
- To get your ideal stance, stand as if trying to tuck your shoulder blades into your back pockets

You'll soon notice your thinking changing. Your mood will improve and you'll look and feel fabulous. You will even look thinner and happier.

Consciously adopting a standing tall position helps you feel strong and confident. This is a great example where making a small change to your body can influence huge changes in your mind and mode of thinking.

In your worn out state you may have noticed that your posture has become slumped, matching your mood. Maybe you have also started to look down at the floor with a dour look on your face. (I did.) It will affect your all-important vibe, how others relate to you and how you relate to the world.

The good news is that this is a simple one to remedy

and can be helped almost instantly.

It doesn't matter if you aren't a particularly tall person either. Improving your posture gives you poise, which in turn will make you appear taller than you actually are.

Poised people are perceived to be more confident, more senior, better at what they do and get more immediate respect. They earn more and are listened to more easily. Oh, and they're apparently perceived as more attractive.

Have you noticed that your posture has matched your mood lately? Have you been a bit slumped all round?

Give yourself a score out of 10 for how often you stand tall.

What do you think about most?

We become what we most think about. All of the great development gurus have come to a similar conclusion.

Your most recent thoughts are influenced by thoughts you had earlier, which were in turn influenced by even earlier thoughts. The contents of your original thoughts were influenced by your experiences and surroundings at that stage and the more you thought about them, the stronger the memories and feelings associated with them. It's no wonder that 'you become what you most think about'.

Thinking is the mental fuel for everything else you do and it is perfectly possible to adjust them with a small amount of mental effort. A focus on good things brings positive results; focus on bad things brings bad results.

Millions of words and thousands of books have been written on this subject. The film '*The Secret*' was all about it and the '*Law of Attraction*' is about it. It has been the culmination of a lifetime's work for gurus who have studied successful people.

You attract what you think about most and that then dominates your thinking and hence your environment.

Think of the people you surround yourself with. Do they stimulate your thinking?

Give yourself a score out of 10.

Do you say thank you?

Do you genuinely thank people when they help you, do a job well, or give good service?

As with helping others, displaying gratitude is another activity that has a wide-ranging impact. You notice, connect, act and learn all at the same time, while nurturing your mental and emotional balance and flexibility. Saying Thank You is also one of those acts where a little effort pays extraordinary dividends.

People love to be noticed and to know that their contribution is recognised. A spot of gratitude will make them feel immediately more favourable towards you and you can usually be assured that the next time they deal with you their performance will be at least as good. You may even recognise that trait in yourself.

On the flip side of the coin, lack of gratitude can rapidly turn people and their opinion against you. As a result, their reaction next time you meet won't necessarily be as favourable or as helpful.

Mind you, you do need to be genuine. Insincere thanks are no thanks at all. A genuine thank you will be clear in your tone of voice, eyes and body language.

It can take years to build a reputation and only a short time to destroy it.

Give yourself an honest score out of 10.

Do you use your eyes, ears and mouth in proportion?

The answer will already be influencing how you connect, learn and notice. It is a critical part of the development of your mental and emotional flexibility and balance.

There is an oft-quoted statistic that 93% of communication between two people is non-verbal — 55% body language and 38% the tone — so it makes sense to look and listen closely.

Actually, it's not quite true. The 55/38/7 proportion (the remaining 7% is down to the words that are used) originates in a combination of two research studies into human communication patterns at UCLA in 1967 and is referred to in the 1971 book 'Silent Messages'.

The studies themselves were very specific. They were about face-to-face encounters and involved subjects saying a total of just ten individual words in three different ways.

The actual conclusion was that these proportions are quite accurate *when the words used are at odds with the body language or the tone of voice being used*. They were never intended to apply to normal conversation or to speeches.

The findings were presented to the media and, as is the way of these things, the message was passed on in ever reducing detail so the 55/38/7 proportion slowly became fact and another new legend was launched into the world.

Notwithstanding that inaccuracy, the principle that non-verbal communication is the most significant element is demonstrated every day in our actions. If in doubt, watch how two people with no language in common can make themselves understood at a simple level.

One of the great skills that the best communicators work hard to develop is active listening — watching and listening very carefully, hearing what is actually being said to them and how it is being said at all times.

If you are talking all the time you are concentrating on your own thoughts so cannot be giving your full attention to the listener. Communication quickly becomes one way. Likewise, if you are listening or watching all the time you may be forming a picture, but unless you talk, communication will be limited. This is where balance comes in.

By keeping eyes, ears and mouth in proportion you enhance communication, and as we are continually told, effective communication is the real success secret.

Score yourself out of 10 on your overall performance in using proportion when you communicate.

Sit and reach

- Sit on the floor with your legs apart in a V shape, the backs of your knees pressing on the floor and your feet against a wall
- Now, keeping your legs straight, reach forwards and touch the floor as far ahead as possible

Log it with a score out of 10. If you prefer a precise measure, count how many centimetres away from the wall you can touch the floor.

This is a really good indicator of flexibility that you can improve on without much effort. It works on the lower back and the hamstrings and is widely used by clinicians to assess if patients could be prone to injury.

If you can already put your nose on the floor between your knees you're in a remarkably good state. Only the most physically flexible people can do this, though, and most of us have scope for improvement. In fact, some people won't even be able to sit up at right angles at first. Your starting point is your individual marker from which to measure your improvement.

You can of course get the same effect by standing up and touching your toes, but everybody does that one. It's nice to be a little bit different, sometimes.

Step into your socks
- Stand up. Hold the sock open
- Without crossing one leg over the other, bring your knee up to your chest and step into the sock
- Repeat with the other sock without falling over.

Can you do it easily with both left and right legs? No, not at the same time, although that would be a great party trick! This is a good test of your flexibility and balance, both of which are important ingredients for your reboot and general wellbeing.

Again, this can be fitted easily into everyday life as it will take less than 10 seconds to improve the overall flexibility of your back, hips and legs. In fact, since most people have to put on socks and pants every day, why not do it this way?

Flexibility, by facilitating movement, helps to stop things hurting – especially the lower back, which is a scourge of many who need to sit for long periods as part of their work.

Each time you get a bit closer to doing it your brain releases a splash of endorphins – the reward chemicals that make you feel good. Success breeds success.

Give yourself a mark out of 10 for how well you managed it. Score zero if you fell flat on your face.

Points to Ponder 1

Are your bits working?
- Establish a baseline so you know your starting point
- Focus on your flexibility, your mind, and your connection with other people
- Your mind and your body are closely interlinked
- Success breeds success
- Small things can have a massive impact
- Keep a log of what you do and how well you do it
- Have fun. It's acceptable

As a reminder, here are the fourteen baseline checks:
- Stand on one leg, eyes closed. Touch nothing
- Step into your socks
- Sit on your heels
- Sit and reach
- Make pictures in your mind
- What's your vibe?
- How do you do? (How do you get on with people?)
- Do you help others?
- Do you say thank you?
- Do you practice being in the moment?
- Do you switch off?
- How often do you really stand tall?
- What do you think about most?
- Do you use eyes, ears and mouth in proportion?

You now have thirteen scores out of 10 PLUS two numbers to indicate how long you were able to stand on either foot with your eyes closed.

If you wish, use these as a baseline and measure them again at the end of your reboot process. You should expect them to change over time, which will provide you with a measurable statistic based on your pown self-honesty and assessment.

Chapter 2 – The Science of Keeping it Simple

"Keep it Simple, Stupid."
Kelly Johnson, Lead Engineer,
Lockheed Skunk Works 1960

While the idea of a reboot is simple, it is based on some very complex neurological and psychological principles.

We have already introduced some concepts key to the effectiveness of a reboot. Working from a baseline; move, connect, give, learn and notice; the butterfly effect; you can affect your body by changing your mind and vice versa...

This chapter introduces four more principles — your brain's plasticity, your neurological reward system, your natural homeostasis and the increasingly recognised nocebo and placebo effects. Being aware that these factors are at work will improve the effect and speed of your reboot.

Please recognise that the concepts are presented here as much-simplified versions of some precise and complex notions. They are used to illustrate how and why the reboot will work for you rather than to try to explain the science to any level of detail.

Neuroplasticity

All of your thoughts, experiences and ideas are held in neural pathways in your brain. That's now a well-established neurological fact. Technically, there's obviously a lot more to it than that, but for now let's try to keep it at a simple level.

For a long time, it was believed that you were born with a finite number of brain cells and when one cell died it wasn't replaced. It was also believed that the creation of new neural pathways started to drop off rapidly at around the age of 20 and then became fixed at around 40.

> Maybe that's why at 20 we knew everything and by 40 we realised how little we actually know.

Here's some good news for anyone over 20: in the last 10-15 years it has been increasingly shown that the brain can create new cells and neural pathways in some areas at any age. It is now an accepted fact that the brain has a plasticity that can be shaped and moulded in a positive direction throughout your life if you encourage it to happen.

Neuroplasticity is the ability of the nervous system - including the brain - to create, reorganise, strengthen or weaken neural pathways. Simplistically, the more neural pathways are used, the thicker and more efficient they get; the less they are used, the weaker they get. Basically, as far as brainpower is concerned, use it or lose it.

The thicker and more efficient those pathways are, the greater their influence on your behaviour, thinking, memories and emotions. Every experience or thought you remember has an effect on the plasticity of your brain. Some pathways are used more than others and so develop; some are unused and so get weaker.

As a point of interest, that means that your brain is different now than it was when you got up this morning entirely due to today's experiences and thoughts.

This happens hand in hand with 'brain pruning', which is the brain eliminating neural connections as we sleep that are rarely or never used. By developing new pathways and clearing away old ones, the brain adapts to the environment it finds itself in.

Sometimes your brain chemistry adapts almost instantaneously, for example to a touch, smell or sound and other times it can take a bit longer to have an effect in one way or another.

Whatever you feed into your mind will develop associated neural pathways and make them stronger. If they are destructive experiences and thoughts, then they will have a negative impact; if they are constructive then they will instantly start to have a positive impact. And you are in control of that choice.

As a practical example: If you attend a one hour lecture on day one and then do nothing with it, by day two you will have forgotten anywhere from 50% to 80% of it, then on every successive day you forget more. By day thirty you will retain only about 2-3% of what you were told.

Things are very different if you use or review it. In doing that you strengthen the neural pathways that were created when you first heard it. If you review the material for just 10 minutes within 24 hours, you will be back to almost 100% retention. If you review it frequently, then a week later it will take only five minutes to reactivate the knowledge; by day 30 you will only need 2-4 minutes to bring back full recall.

So what?

Throughout this book you may notice some techniques that work with your brain's plasticity. You can take charge of directing your brain to work the way you want it to.

Use it or lose it.

The Reward system

The reward system is a brain network that rewards you with pleasurable feelings if you are successful at a task that requires a bit of effort.

It rewards certain 'behaviours', which encourages you to repeat it. Good behaviour, of course, is that which is good for your overall body. (Comment added from clinician reviewer: "Not always. It also rewards addiction". Noted. This is true.)

It may help to provide a little bit of background to illustrate this.

Neural pathways work by sending messages between neurons, a bit like an electrical circuit in your home. However, neurons don't touch each other. Instead to send a message, a neuron releases a chemical (neurotransmitter) into the space (synapse) between it and the next cell. The neurotransmitter fills the synapse and attaches to proteins (receptors) on the receiving brain cell. This causes changes in the receiving neuron – the message is delivered. The more often this is done, the stronger the pathway.

Comment from clinician: "What is often referred to as a brain cell is actually made up of a blob that is the cell plus a strand going out of it that is the neuron." Clarity does help.

There are four major neurotransmitters in the brain

that influence our happiness – dopamine, oxytocin, serotonin and endorphins.

Dopamine — often called the striving drug — is generated through anticipation of achievement. It makes you feel mentally alert, bright and energised. It is created just before the point of achievement and is a major element in the reward system.

Oxytocin — also known as the cuddle hormone — another element of the reward system is released through closeness to other people. That can be physical, but in a professional environment is more likely to be through attentiveness, eye contact or mental or social bonding.

Serotonin — the happiness hormone — controls your greater mood and calms you down. It is also an analgesic. If you're in a great mood, be thankful for having plenty of serotonin; if you're in a mean and bad-tempered mood or even mildly depressed, that will be down to a shortage. About 80%-90% of serotonin is made in your gut, so the fuel you use will of course affect it, as does walking in sunshine and nature.

Endorphins are pain relievers and will help you to experience fewer of the negative effects of stress. The word endorphin is a contraction of 'endogenous morphine' which means they are our natural morphine. Being natural they are far more powerful and have no side effects. Endorphins can lead to short sensations of euphoria and high excitement.

So what?

In the reboot there are activities aimed at stimulating production of some of these special chemicals. Let's not pretend they can be targeted with great precision, but what we're after is the general effect.

For example, if you do a bit of exercise that gets the blood pumping around your body and your body and muscles moving as they were designed to do, that is naturally good for you. Billions of your brain cells natter away to each other saying "Good on you". Of course, they have to pass the message from cell to cell and so more and more of these chemicals are required. You feel great as a result.

The reward system is a great thing for getting and keeping us going.

Homeostasis

Balance really matters to us humans.

Your physical body is a masterpiece of intricately and finely balanced engineering and homeostasis is the process of how it keeps a stable and constant internal environment by self-regulating everything that goes on at all times. For example, if you are in a cold environment, your body naturally stops sweating and reduces blood circulation to the skin.

Homeostasis is a natural state of balance when an organism is healthy and homeostatic reactions are inevitable if the system is actually functioning optimally. The natural state of your bodily system is in balance.

On balance, homeostasis is A Good Thing.

However, for a professional's psyche, the desire to 'stay balanced' can encourage you to stay well within your 'comfort zone'.

The 'comfort zone' is a psychological state where you feel comfortable, in control, familiar and at ease, each of which is a good life goal in itself and to be encouraged at all times.

Alas, your desire to stay in your comfort zone can play havoc with your personal and professional development, stifle ideas and suffocate ambition. When you stay in the comfort zone without trying to push the boundaries even a little bit, you will end up using only a limited set of repeated behaviours. You stop taking risks, you stop growing and you gradually stop trying new or different things.

You end up inflexible in an environment where flexibility and balance are two of the most important factors for successfully climbing out of that hole and moving on.

Many professionals looking for a reboot find that they have gradually slipped into a zone that is a bit too comfortable, leaning on habits that have formed through repetition over extended periods of time. Repeated use means, of course, that the neural pathways associated with the behaviours and thoughts are thick and efficient, so the links will be powerful. The introduction of regular novelty is essential for growing new pathways and a healthy brain environment.

So what?

For your reboot programme, be aware of the importance and value of homeostasis. At the same time, recognise the dangers of the comfort zone and the fact that feeling comfortable is so pleasant that it can become necessary to make active mental and emotional effort to move forwards.

Nocebos

Most people have heard of the idea of a placebo and the placebo effect. A placebo (Latin translation: 'I will please') is an agent — usually a medicine or procedure — that has a mental rather than a physical effect on a patient. It appears to be a genuine treatment but in reality is not.

The *placebo effect* happens when a positive outcome results from a seemingly inert agent or activity.

A *placebo* is a medicine or procedure that has a positive effect on you but at this moment in time we cannot explain how.

The use of placebos always presents the ethical debate about whether the patient should be told about it or not because that could affect the patient expectations.

Placebos are widely used in clinical trials to establish a control group against which the impacts of a 'proper' treatment can be assessed. The placebo effect occurs when there is a positive benefit to a patient that is not attributable to the fake pill or treatment. Placebo effects have been reported in 21% to 40%, even as high as 60% of subjects with certain conditions depending upon the study type. That's a success level quite close to, or better than, many prescription drugs in recent years.

It can also add to the effectiveness of a known drug. For example, it is well known in medical circles that the drug paracetamol is more effective when taken in a red and blue capsule rather than as a white tablet. Nobody knows why.

Many professionals naturally use the equivalent of a placebo at some point in their work. Tidy presentation, a smile, timeliness and politeness all combine to give the impression of competence even before you have done anything; the use of top quality tools and materials sets others apart; some clinicians still use the white coat and complex charts to encourage belief; physiotherapists for football teams have long used the magic sponge to cure players almost immediately, despite their writhing around on the floor in apparent agony after a gentle challenge.

At the other extreme there is the nocebo effect. This is relevant to you.

The *nocebo effect* (Latin translation: 'I will harm') comes about when patients taking medicines experience adverse side effects unrelated to the drug due to their expectations and conditioning. In comparison to the placebo effect, the nocebo effect has been relatively obscure until recently.

Here we should add in an powerful comment from

a clinician: "Language alone can also be a nocebo. It doesn't have to include drugs.". As usual, that's very true. I have recently been involved in a short study of the language used by some medical clinicians and the impact it has on patients. It's incredible what you hear and it's really no surprise that you see some patients head downhill after a diagnosis.

Nocebos work because of negative expectation and it is only recently that scientists have begun to recognise the significance of its impact. When a patient expects things to go wrong it can cause even the best treatments to fail.

A slightly wider definition is where negative expectations are encouraged or planted as a result of the careless use of language or poor preparation. Some professionals who are operating from deep inside their comfort zone fall into this self-made trap.

So what?

As you go through your reboot, look to identify any nocebos in your life and sort them out. Be prepared for some surprises, too. They are disconcertingly common. Cutting out negative expectations at the start gives every activity a greater chance of success.

Points to Ponder 2

A reboot is simple. The science and psychology behind it are highly complex.
- Your brain has a plasticity that can be moulded and shaped at every stage of your life. It changes with every experience, thought or memory you have
- The more you use your brain, the stronger your associated neural pathways become
- Brain pruning eliminates unused neural pathways. Use it or lose it
- Chemicals such as dopamine and oxytocin regulate your emotions and feelings. You can target production of these chemicals with special actions
- Homeostasis is A Good Thing when it means that your body maintains a stable and constant internal environment. It means you are well
- A desire to stay balanced is A Bad Thing when it is used as a justification to stay well inside your comfort zone and avoid risk, growth and development
- The nocebo effect is the opposite of the placebo effect. Eliminating nocebos from your environment increases the speed at which you get back on track.

STEP 2 – Load Your 'Operating System'

*One of the first Operating System files
is a file such as CONFIG.SYS.
Information in this file tells which
specific drivers are to be launched.
Another special file tells which applications
or commands the user wants to have
included as part of the boot process.
In Windows, this is called WIN.INI.*

*OR: What guides and drives you?
What are your rules?*

Chapter 3 – The Real You

*"Today you are You, that is truer than true.
There is no-one alive who is Youer than You"*
Dr. Seuss

What makes up your 'Operating System'? What is the combination of rules and goals that consciously and unconsciously guide your life? What makes You You?

Step 1 was all about establishing a baseline.

Step 2 is to remind yourself where you have come from, where you are going and the rules that you live by. This knowledge will enable you to expand on your 'where am I now?' baseline.

What influences your decisions and how much flexibility do you allow yourself? Getting some clarity will help you to target and enjoy this reboot even more.

The home of Australia's parliament in Canberra is underground. Well, to be precise, it is built where a hill used to be then the hill was plopped back on top once the building work was finished. That's so that the building 'can symbolically rise out of the Australian landscape as true democracy rises from the state of things.'

If you decide to visit it, you can find out how to get there by having just two pieces of information –

precisely where you are right now and the place you want to get to.

The details of how you will make the journey can then be planned and adjusted as you go along.

It's the same when you embark on any new project or activity: know your start and desired end positions and you can map out a route to follow.

If either of those two are missing then you are dependent on guesswork.

Now you could try out guesswork occasionally for a bit of fun as it can actually encourage exploration and creative thinking by pushing you out of your comfort zone. After all, there's little more exciting than firefighting and flying by the seat of your pants because you get immediate feedback after a pressurised period. However, it soon wears you down if you're doing it all the time.

For the professional, it doesn't often work to lurch from one reactive crisis to another. Which, of course, may be exactly where you are now. When you're feeling a bit worn out, it helps to have a framework you can rely on.

In this step, spend a bit of time reminding yourself where you have come from and where you are going. Sometimes those guides can get lost in the general busy-ness of life. We want to resurrect them here so it will be worth the effort to take a bit of time to think about these things.

It will be easier if you identify and concentrate on the positive perspectives. It is the easiest – or is it really the laziest? – thing in the world to whinge and whine and point out the negatives. That's why many people do just that. Being flexible and creative in your thinking enables you to recognise more possibilities.

It is considerably more constructive and helpful to concentrate on the good things. Yes, problems happen, yet dwelling on them rarely helps. Acknowledge them, do what you need to do to resolve or accept them, then move on. Bitching and moaning poison your mind and starve your ability to think flexibly. You can comfortably do without them. Instead, positivity and flexibility are much more productive fuels.

If you load your Operating System with the emphasis on optimism then you are building a good, solid foundation. By apparently sheer coincidence you will also find that good things will start to happen. Gary Player famously said: "The more I practice, the luckier I get". You'll find that happens to you, too. What goes around, comes around.

Identify your foundations, key influences and your cornerstone principles. Once you have reminded yourself of yours they will provide a guiding light to keep everything else you do in perspective. You achieved your level of success thanks to these drivers, so remind yourself what they are and what gave you your initial enthusiasm and 'joie de vivre'.

The cornerstone is the first stone set in a building's foundations. All other stones will be set in reference to this stone, thus determining the position of the entire structure. The placing of every subsequent stone contributes to the overall construction where each has its own place in relation to the others and individually adds to the overall strength and beauty.

This chapter identifies your own cornerstone. It's all about you.

It can help if you think of your 'self' as a balanced series of building blocks. Each experience you have ever had, major or minor, has contributed to getting you to where you are right now. Every decision, triumph, correct call and mistake has been based on what went before and together they have built up to shape your entirely unique life.

There are five key questions in Step 2. Take a bit of time to consider them. Remind yourself of the good things that have got you to where you are today and that will influence where you go. Recall the challenges that you have faced to get where you are now, because they are the experiences that really forged you and made you what you are now.

Be glad to be good, take pride in your morals and ethics because they are good.

If you are keeping a log, it will be useful to take notes as you work through this part of the process. Your thoughts will all add up to make your framework a solid, self-supporting structure rather than a Jenga™-like stack that can tumble and crash if the wrong brick is disturbed.

Finally, let's emphasise again – this reboot isn't about creating a new life plan or changing the way you relate to the world. You can do them later if you want to. This is about a quick kick-start to move you from feeling down to up.

This step is simply about identifying your key influences and appreciating them.

What's your story?

Everybody has their own story to tell – especially you as a professional. You have worked hard and encountered all sorts of challenges to get to where you are now. It is a powerful exercise to remember your own story: there are over seven billion people in the world and nobody has a story like yours.

Where did you come from? What made you what you are? What gives you your buzz? What caused you to start along the path to become the professional you are? And what kept you in balance on that path even when the going got tough?

Give yourself five minutes and take a deep breath to quickly gather the information, then tell your story. Close your eyes and let your memory transport you to each key moment and imagine you are experiencing it again. It can be highly instructive if you say your story out loud, record it on your phone and listen to it. The words you use, the tone and the sometimes-unconscious emphases will tell a story in themselves.

In the story, identify the key people, the turning points and the major challenges you overcame. Identify the connections, the major lessons, your health and fitness and the greatest gifts and kindnesses you received. Write your story down, record it or simply relate it to somebody important to you who will listen to it closely and confidentially.

A powerful extension of your story is to go through it again, reminding yourself of all the successes that you have clocked up on the way to where you are. Look for the positive slant rather than bemoaning errors. Focus on the 96% that went right, then remind yourself how you dealt with the problems brought in by the 4% that went wrong.

It is often said that the only things we truly learn from are our mistakes so if you cannot get beyond thinking about that 4%, identify the things you learned that resulted in your success to date then appreciate them for the gems they are.

For example, this is how I found out about this fascinating and effective technique...

My story – Going Dutch

I first met Anneke at a workshop I was running. Early talk over dinner at the end of a long day revolved around the football World Cup that was going on at the time. She was following the fortunes of the Dutch team closely, which provided a mutual interest as I was doing a lot of work in Holland at the time.

At one point during the meal, she suddenly said out of nowhere: "So tell me: Where did you come from? What got you to where you are?" She was probably asking a couple of simple questions just to keep the conversation moving, but they had a surprising effect on my mindset.

I was actually taken aback because nobody had ever asked me that before, so I had never really thought about it. The timing was especially relevant to me for a number of personal and professional reasons so maybe I was subconsciously already tuned in to the idea. We are all normally too busy looking after our own business. And she actually seemed to be interested in the answer, too!

I had just a few seconds to come up with a reply. Images and feelings from my life quickly tumbled into my mind and aligned themselves ready. I instinctively felt that my words would be significant in learning about myself. I needed to be brief yet give enough information to tell the story and identify the really key turning points.

It was clear that my father's attitude was significant. He adored his work as a teacher in a school in a deprived area and got such a buzz helping the kids to develop against the odds that it infused his every action. My memory was of him bouncing home each day with a huge grin exclaiming "This isn't work! AND I get paid!"

I realised that had affected my own approach to work throughout my life and that it had influenced many career and life decisions.

I then quickly identified a handful of real turning points in my life. There was the day I decided to leave school rather than stay behind to improve on my results, despite Tom's efforts; there were the two phone calls 10 years apart with Jo and with Pete that completely changed the direction and tone of my career and life; there was the day that (big — very big) Les decided that I would play rugby instead of carrying on with soccer; there was the day that Hargreaves set me up on a blind date with the girl who became my wife; and there was the day I realised I had missed five years' worth of my kids growing up. Even writing about them now has set my spine tingling.

They all led to my making big decisions that aused enormous changes in my life.

It took less than five minutes before I could ask Anneke the same questions. It was an extraordinarily effective way to identify my real drivers. Try it.

Holland didn't win the World Cup, but I got a marvellous tool to help my personal and professional development. Now it's yours. I'm passing it on to you.

Here's another nice example of a story...

Vince's story

Vince Molinaro knows exactly when his career direction became clear. In his first job out of college, he loved the work but the atmosphere was unexciting as people just went through the motions. He said he remembered thinking, "Is this it? Is this what working in the real world is like?"

A senior manager named Zinta realised that Vince wanted to change things a bit and invited him to join a group of other colleagues to seek and implement ideas for a more positive environment in work. They began to make small changes, and attitudes gradually changed.

Then Zinta was diagnosed with a serious illness and without her there to discourage it, the old culture slowly returned. On a visit Vince told her about the change in attitude. She commented that since she had never smoked and there was no history of cancer in her family, she believed that her disease was a direct function of having to work within and putting up with a toxic work environment for so long.

Later Zinta sent Vince a letter telling him he would be faced with an important choice throughout his life. He could allow the negative attitudes of others to influence his behaviour, or pursue professional goals because of the sense of personal accomplishment they offered. That letter changed Vince's life, inspiring him to leave his job and start his own consulting business devoted to helping people be better leaders.

Everybody has their story. What's yours?

What are your values?

> *"Keep your thoughts positive because
> your thoughts become your words.
> Keep your words positive because
> your words become your behaviour.
> Keep your behaviour positive because
> your behaviour becomes your habits.
> Keep your habits positive because*
>
> *your habits become your values.
> Keep your values positive because
> your values become your destiny."*
> Mahatma Gandhi

What is important to you? Your values are the criteria that you use to make major decisions in every aspect of your life.

What are your values?
- If you have any that you tend to rely on, write them down
- Now prioritise them to identify the most dominant one. What is the one value that overrides all others?
- Finally, ask yourself how closely you live your life to your values. There is nothing so energising or good for the self as living life by your values without compromise.

Your values define you. The way you apply them defines you even further. They are your conscience, your moral compass and are always unconsciously and consciously referred to when making any significant decision. They emerge from your background, experiences and the environment you live in. They are reflected in everything you do and are the backbone of your life. Despite this very few of us ever take the time to identify them.

Any time you are in a situation that you are not comfortable with, it usually means that some of your values are being compromised.

Business has long used value sets to give guidance to employees, customers and suppliers. It is always an interesting exercise to review a company's website and read their stated values.

On the next two pages are the value sets for some of the world's most influential companies. They make thought-provoking reading. Compare how they relate to the move, connect, give, learn and notice themes. Values give a real insight into a company.

Google

Focus on the user and all else will follow
It's best to do one thing really, really well
Fast is better than slow
Democracy on the web works
You don't need to be at your desk to need an answer
You can make money without doing evil
There's always more information out there
The need for information crosses all borders
You can be serious without a suit
Great just isn't good enough

Barnes & Noble Booksellers

Customer Service
Quality
Empathy
Respect
Integrity
Responsibility
Teamwork

IBM

Dedication to every client's success
Innovation that matters for our company
and for the world
Trust and personal responsibility in all relationships

The Coca Cola company

"Our values serve as a compass for our actions and describe how we behave in the world."

Leadership: The courage to shape a better future

Collaboration: Leverage collective genius

Integrity: Be real

Accountability: If it is to be, it's up to me

Passion: Committed in heart and mind

Diversity: As inclusive as our brands

Quality: What we do, we do well

Microsoft

Our Values

As a company, and as individuals, we value integrity, honesty, openness, personal excellence, constructive self-criticism, continual self-improvement, and mutual respect. We are committed to our customers and partners and have a passion for technology. We take on big challenges, and pride ourselves on seeing them through. We hold ourselves accountable to our customers, shareholders, partners, and employees by honouring our commitments, providing results, and striving for the highest quality.

What are your goals?

We all have goals in one form or another although sometimes it can feel as though they have been either forgotten or converted to the status of 'unrealistic wish', submerged by life..

What are yours? Try this little exercise:

- Spend a short time reminding yourself what your goals are. Recall all those short, medium and long term ideas that you have been thinking over because they may have slipped out of your immediate memory
- Next – write them down. About 95% of the population omit this step. Doing this immediately places you in the 5% more likely to succeed
- Now, as you did with your values, prioritise them and identify your number one goal from your existing list.

Look at them and remind yourself why you chose them.

Goals are what give your life purpose and everybody has them even if they may have slipped below the radar for a short while. Goals are your dreams, hopes and aspirations that get you through the tough times and raise your spirits when you're wondering what life is all about. They are what you hold onto when times are tough.

The act of writing them down will almost certainly produce some conflicting thoughts and debate in your mind. Avoid the temptation to create new goals. That is for another time.

For the purposes of the reboot this exercise is to bring out into the open any existing goals or dreams you have. It is about reminding yourself where you are going and whether that is consistent with other things you are doing in your life.

Start at the end. What's your eulogy?

Imagine you are attending a funeral service, packed to the rafters with people. Beyond the inevitable sadness of the occasion, there is a shared pride at having known the deceased. People share anecdotes with smiles and fondness. It is a happy occasion. Watch it as if through the eyes of one of the attendees and listen carefully to what is being said.

After a while you realise that you are attending your own funeral.

In your ideal world, what would be getting said about you? What is the feeling in the room? How do people remember you?

Write your own eulogy. This is a suggestion from Steven Covey in his seminal book *'Seven Habits of Highly Effective People'*. Start at the end. It brings focus to the mind.

As with the other exercises in this step, this can produce some interesting results as it leads you to consider where your life is heading. It may be that things are not going as you would like. Equally, it may be that everything is actually pretty darn good and that your current mood or feeling is a temporary lull in your onward progress towards destiny. There can be some life affirming changes in attitude as a result of mentally attending your own funeral.

If you don't like what's being said in your mental story – change it. You are imagining a future event and you have absolute power and flexibility to influence it. In making the changes in your thoughts, the new opinion will be fed into your subconscious and, if the feeling is strong enough, it will begin to impact the way you lead your life.

Do you remember the Ghandi quote a few pages back? The way you work and carry yourself fuels your destiny. Remember that in your thoughts and deeds.

Write your own eulogy. Even if you end up changing your mind about some of the detail at a later date in the light of experience, it will give an indication of some of your core hopes and dreams.

Do you have attitude?

> *"It isn't what you have or who you are*
> *or where you are or what you are doing*
> *that makes you happy or unhappy.*
> *It is what you think about it."*
> Dale Carnegie

Earl Nightingale calls it "the magic word". The topic of attitudes was first introduced in Step 1 with the question about your personal vibe. You are the only one who can control your attitude. Others may do things that affect it, but only you can change it. Most people live each day allowing their subconscious, reactive side to determine theirs. Consciously choose your attitude each day for a week. The impact can be magical.

Doing so can literally transform the way you interact with the world around you. And you alone have the power to choose it.

Your attitude is the single most effective aspect of your personality, influencing everything you do and everybody you meet. Your personal vibe, if you like.

I really relate to this passage by Earl Nightingale:

> *"If you develop and hold an attitude that says 'yes' to life it encourages a positive, solution-focused mindset that will show up in the way you behave towards others. You will quickly notice things changing, especially your 'luck'. Irritations disappear; people respond differently; emotions of*

anger, hatred and jealousy that only cause damage will be replaced by emotions of love, appreciation, gratitude and enjoyment."

It sounds a bit hippy, yes, but many years' experience confirms it to be overwhelmingly true.

Your enthusiasm will grow and very quickly you will feel a boost of positive energy that will be to everybody's benefit and appreciation.

It is your attitude more than anything else that will determine the level of success you achieve in any activity. It affects your determination and willingness to go that extra mile and it influences the way you think and the approach you take in every circumstance. That, in turn, influences how others react to you and it becomes self-fulfilling.

Your world and environment reflect your attitude. If you think in negative terms, you tend to get a negative response. Expect good things of yourself and others and it emerges in your attitude and personal vibe. You'll find that you live up to your expectations and others raise their game to meet them too. You get back what you put out. What goes around comes around.

There is a marvellous example of selecting attitudes in the book 'Fish'. To cut a short story even shorter, work in one business in Seattle was dreary and unexciting, so people were shown an environment filled with positive attitude and given a choice. A team suggested having different attitudes as a menu on a two-sided coin and people could, if they wished, toss the coin to select an attitude each day.

On the one side was a smiley face ☺ with words like 'energy', 'quality', 'caring', 'helpful', 'happy', 'cheerful'. On the other was a miserable face ☹ with words like 'dull', 'dour', 'angry', 'fed up', 'disinterested', 'grumpy'. Remember nocebos?

I know which type I'd rather be and be with!

It certainly helps to experiment with variations:
− Imagine that you are the most successful person in the world.
  Notice what happens. Are you standing taller, acting calmer and getting more respect? Are you open with people? Do you learn from your experiences?
− Try an attitude that is wholly positive, as suggested by Earl Nightingale.
  Carrying the attitude that says 'The answer is Yes. Now, what's the question?' has extraordinary powers that will draw like-minded people to you and encourage a constructive environment.
  To which we should add a useful note from a Wellness consultant: "At the same time, be wary

of becoming a doormat. The word 'No' when used correctly can be highly positive too. After all, if you never say 'No', what value does your 'Yes' have?"

- Try an attitude of gratitude for a week.
  Say thank you when someone helps you and show appreciation for a job well done. You will already have a baseline log of how often you say thank you, so work to build on this score.
- At the end of each day list down some of the things that you are thankful to have. Dwell on each of them for a short while at the end of each day or just before you go to sleep. If you get a chance and are willing, share them with someone else.
  The things you are grateful for can be minor. The pleasant conversation you had, the closeness of a friendship, the kind act that someone did for you, the tone of colour of a piece of clothing, the smile you got from that person on the train, the taste of that meal, the tingling feeling after a good bit of exercise….

I strongly recommend that you write down each item you are thankful for in your log. They will have added significance when you go back to read them at different points in the future. Let's move on…

"Everything can be taken from a man but one thing: the last of the human freedoms – to choose one's attitude in any given set of circumstances, to choose one's own way."

Viktor E Frankl, Man's Search for Meaning

Points to Ponder 3

Who is the real you? What makes You You?
- Having established a baseline, get clarity in what guides and drives you
- Identify your foundations, cornerstones and key influences along the way
- Undertake a review with optimism – it's a lot easier
- There is nothing so energising or good for the self as living life by your values without compromise
- Your values define you. They are your moral compass
- Goals are what give your life purpose and interest
- Consciously choose your attitude each day

There are just five key questions in Chapter 3. Take time to consider them.
- What's your story?
- What are your values?
- What are your goals?
- What's your eulogy?
- Do you have a useful attitude?

STEP 3 – Load Services

After all 'Operating System' files have been loaded, they are given control of the computer and perform a set of initial commands. These include loading up 'Services', which are little applications that run in the background.

Big programs can take a while to load. By running a 'Service' in the background, shared components can be pre-loaded and run continuously. That way they're ready when they're needed.

OR: This is your toolkit

Chapter 4 – Quick Wins

"Each of us is like that butterfly in the Butterfly Effect. And each tiny move towards a positive mindset can send ripples of positivity through our organisations, our families and our communities"
Shawn Achor

Krav Maga is an astonishingly effective self defence system. It was originally developed for the Israeli military and is now the system of choice for U.S. military units and law enforcement agencies all over the world.

Krav Maga s an instant, explosive and extremely violent triple response to an attack. Bam! Bam! Bam! The key is in its immediate impact which creates space and time to develop a strategy for what to do next. The quick, sharp activity provides a massive stimulus to the body and mind and gets results quickly.

Even a relatively small response exerted rapidly can have an enormous effect.

Having a set of quick acting actions to hand will help you too. The following 32 tricks and techniques will all provide an immediate boost to your energy levels. Some of them are dramatic and some of them are quite subtle. Use them to raise your "RAH!" quotient when you need to.

They will all result in quick and easy wins for you. They take little effort and will have a striking effect. They all work and have been tried and tested in many and varied environments.

Any of these can trigger the 'Butterfly Effect' mentioned in the 'Just how DO you get going again' section earlier in the book. Combine them with a positive attitude and the chances of outstanding results will be multiplied.

Talk Loudly

The number one tip that always works to quickly generate energy and oomph: Talk louder, a bit faster and add enthusiasm and emphasis to your voice.

Adding volume to your speech encourages the enthusiasm; upping the pace whips up the energy. It can also add significantly to your confidence.

It is an incredibly simple technique and it works – even when you're feeling low.

You will also find that this works to raise the tempo and energy in an audience if you are presenting. Raise your voice. Talk loudly. The difference can be extraordinary.

'Do' – Even If It Is Just One Thing

Nothing ever happens without action. All success needs action. You may be feeling low because of the absence of success. Lack of success leads to passivity and so a cycle of inactivity and diminishing success is created. So create your own success.

Simply taking one practical step towards an end result – no matter how small – energises and will switch your mindset from idle to active. The very act of crossing an item off a 'to-do' list is a success and will give you a little rush of energy. Real success comes from a whole load of little successes one after the other.

Solving a problem or doing a puzzle successfully will stimulate a feel-good sensation that cannot help but energise you.

Big effects can emerge from small changes. Work with the principle that anything that moves your mindset towards the positive causes the brain to produce the chemicals that produce that feel-good rush.

Write Down Your Good Points

Yes, you do have good points and many of them. This is a classic technique used in 'therapy' or to raise your self-esteem. Write down seven things you like about yourself. An increase in self confidence has a remarkable effect on your energy in the same way as an increase in physical energy does.

In the late 1990s a teacher asked everybody in her sixth-grade class to write down something they liked about each of their classmates. The teacher then pulled the comments together, removed the names and one by one handed the lists to each pupil. What an affect it had on the children! Their confidence and academic performances soared and the group stayed much closer than normal class groups through their schooling.

Years later many of them reassembled for the funeral of one of their number who had joined the forces and died in conflict. In his pocket he had been carrying his list. It turned out that most of the group who attended the funeral had always made a point of carrying their lists with them almost every day.

It helps to list your good points.

Smile

> *"Smiling people are mentally, psychologically and physically healthier."*
> Dr. T.P Chia

Smiling really ought to be everybody's activity of choice. It releases endorphins, natural pain killers and serotonin and together these make you feel wonderful. It is quick to take effect and makes people around you feel happy too. In fact, we humans are wired to respond like for like so find it hard to respond to a smile with a frown.

A study in Sweden in 2002 showed that people respond in kind to the facial expressions they encounter. They instinctively wanted to reflect what they'd been exposed to, answering smile for smile and frown for frown, and could not easily overcome this urge even when they were quite consciously trying.

Any time you feel down or worn out, smile – even if you don't feel like it. Grin for all you are worth for a full minute and the very act of smiling will change your mood.

Alternatively, try this approach: Smile quickly with your mouth 10 times in a row. Very quickly. Don't worry about getting your eyes involved – that may occur naturally by the end.

The French physician Guillaume Duchenne first

identified how to spot a genuine smile. Because of the muscles used, a genuine or 'Duchenne' smile causes the eyes to close, crow's feet to appear at the edge of the eyes and in most cases hides the lower set of teeth.

You will notice a pleasant tingling sensation spreading through your head and down towards your shoulders. You will start to feel good.

Earlier in the book there was the example of imagining standing on top of the tallest crane without any support to demonstrate how changing your mindset can affect your physiology. This is an example of the reverse effect – changing your physiology can change your mindset. Regardless of your mood at the start, your body and your mind will feel different having smiled.

This simple act has this almost magical effect even if you're feeling down. It has the power to lift your sense of sadness and wash your blues away.

A smiling person lightens up a room, lifting the mood of all around them. Try it. It will make you feel happier in the process too. You will draw people to you because smiles are contagious and encourage people to smile themselves.

When you smile you are sending your brain a message that 'Life is Good!' and your mindset moves towards the positive. In fact, it is quite difficult to think of something negative while you are smiling. Try it. It's easier to stay cheerful.

Smiling also 'lifts' your facial muscles, helping you to look less tired or stressed, even younger. It helps your immune system to work better and lowers your blood pressure too.

That's a lot of benefits from a something as simple as a smile.

"A smile costs nothing but gives much.
It enriches those who receive without making poorer those who give. It takes but a moment, but the memory of it sometimes lasts forever.
None is so rich or mighty that he cannot get along without it and none is so poor that he cannot be made rich by it.
Yet a smile cannot be bought, begged, borrowed, or stolen, for it is something that is of no value to anyone until it is given away.
Some people are too tired to give you a smile. Give them one of yours, as none needs a smile so much as he who has no more to give."
Author Unknown

Look Fabulous

When you make an effort to look good, you feel better about yourself. And feeling better about yourself gives you more energy.

So put some effort into looking your very best. Wear tidy clothes, stand tall and breathe deeply. You will actually feel a boost in confidence and energy.

Hey, you may even get some compliments! And honest compliments really are energising.

Eat Chocolate

You get an endorphin buzz from chocolate and an energy boost from the little bit of caffeine that chocolate contains. Dark chocolate is good for you because it has more cocoa and caffeine and fewer fats than milk chocolate.

Flavonoids found in cocoa have been shown to improve mood and boost cognitive skills. The higher the cocoa content, the higher the flavonoid content, the higher the benefits. Some studies have even shown that dark chocolate can reduce blood pressure, 'bad' cholesterol and is good for the heart. It's healthy in moderation.

Well, to be really precise, two or three squares (37g) of high quality, high cocoa content dark chocolate are good for you if you consume them occasionally. However, one square is enough to give you the benefits without upping your calorie content significantly so you could indulge in one every day.

Mirror And Pace

Mirroring works to raise your mood by giving somebody else your attention, listening and noticing what they do and how they do it. In additional, you will develop a closer connection with the other person.

- Start a conversation with someone
- Now add a bit of enthusiasm to your voice, increase the speed you talk at and add a little to the volume
- Notice how they start to talk a bit louder and a bit faster themselves. As you match them the energy and volume of whole conversation will soar.

Your extra enthusiasm will subconsciously persuade your conversation partner to match you and raise the levels a little. It's that 'Law of Reciprocity' in action. The added enthusiasm also quickly persuades them – once again, unwittingly – to match or reflect your actions, voice tones and body language. Throw in a few smiles and they'll replicate those too.

This is a great exercise for starting a meeting or a workshop. Pair people off with the simple instruction to start talking cheerfully and to mirror the other person. It has a remarkable effect on the atmosphere and energy in the room.

Enthusiasm is contagious and highly energising.

Splash Water On Your Face

This can energise you even faster than other options like drinking coffee, or so said one study reported in the *'Journal of Clinical Neurophysiology'*.

It's not quite as extreme or immersive as leaping into the frigidarium as the Romans used to do to stir themselves, or combining cold and hot baths as top sports people use to aid recovery, but it works to give a quick boost. It's all about changing the flow of blood.

Stand Up And Smile While You Dial

There is no end to the benefits of smiling. A smile can even have an effect on others over the phone!

This is a classic standard of sales and telesales training courses around the world and has been shown to be highly effective over decades.

You can 'hear' a smile on the telephone. When you smile you come across as interesting and enthusiastic to the person who you called. They recognise the smile in your voice and are naturally drawn to it.

Mind you, take care not to be over-cheesy, though!

You can add considerably to the effect by standing up. When you stand up to make a phone call you feel more confident and focused on the call. Your attention is drawn to the person at the other end.

If you have ever been to a meeting where all the chairs have been taken out of the room, you may remember how energetic the meeting was and how well everybody kept to the agenda. It's a well-established way to make meetings stay focused and it works wonderfully well.

Standing up gives you energy and adds to your focus. It also helps to negate the detrimental effects of sitting down for extended periods. So, get up and give a happy smile while you dial.

Have a Short Burst Of Activity

When you need some instant 'RAH!' engage in a bit of physical activity to get the blood flowing and your heart pumping harder than usual.

Physical activity increases your circulation, relieves muscle tension and causes your brain to release endorphins. It also means you take in more oxygen and your metabolism gets fired up – all within just a minute or two rom the start.

Try any of these short bursts of activity for a couple of minutes to generate instant energy. There is also plenty of scope here for some play, which is a great way to generate additional enthusiasm.

- March in place
- Glide around the room as if you're on skates
- Trot or walk up and down a set of stairs
- Skip along a corridor
- Run around with kids. Enthusiasm in a tiny package
- Jump up and touch the ceiling
- Dance. It's joyful even (or necessary in my case!) on your own
- Do 10 quick press-ups against a doorframe
- Clap your hands 30 times in 10 seconds
- Quickly rock from your toes to your heels. The rhythm builds the energy

As you move you'll soon start to feel that vital energy rising up inside you. It's simple and very exciting.

Play Loud Music

The pleasure centres in your brain light up when you hear the right type of music. In the right environment it can also boost your energy and productivity.

All you need to do is to increase the volume and your spirits will soar with the beat and rhythm. Mind you, make sure you respect the people around you and don't disturb them.

Listening to music and tapping their toes significantly increased college kids' alertness in one survey and a report in the 'Online Journal of Sport Psychology' said that loud music may be one of the most effective tools for relieving stress and fighting fatigue.

No shit, Sherlock. So there's some evidence to support what you have always known. For further evidence, watch any line of traffic and it is certain that at least one vehicle will have the volume up, the passengers feeding off the rhythm.

Having said that, note a caution from one reviewer: "There is also some research that listening to music can distract attention, especially if it has lyrics. While it may be great for raising your mood it may not help with concentration, accuracy or driving safely." OK

For greater effect, listen to tunes that start slowly and build to a crescendo. They are designed to deliberately carry your spirit up and down through a series of emotions before building to a soaring climax.

Create a personal playlist of music that raises your spirits and switch it on whenever you need it. It will switch you back on too.

Howl At The Moon

Sometimes it helps to simply release tension with a controlled blast of energy. The important word here is 'controlled'.

The explosive release of a loud shout releases a rush of dopamine and you'll feel a zap of excitement. Roar very loudly or scream at the moon and you will feel your vocal chords jangling accompanied by a flood of feel-good chemicals.

Take A Hot Bath, Shower Or Sauna

The extremes of heat and the sensation of water on your skin stimulate the mind and body. According to one UK study up to 68% of men feel more energised after a hot bath or shower. So that means that it's got a two in three chance of working for you.

Similarly, cold showers stimulate the circulatory system and the metabolism and leave you with a feeling that you are alive and alert.

Saunas – whether including an ice bath after sitting in a hot room or just enjoying the heat treatment – are invigorating, refreshing and highly energising at the same time as being deeply relaxing and calming. No wonder the good citizens of Finland love them so much.

Sing

Sing. Just sing. Belt a tune out as if you were leading the world in chorus. Car drivers do it all the time, people in showers do it, sports supporters by the million do it. Up until early this century many companies still began their day with a rendition of the 'Company Song'.

> Company Songs were sung to energise the workers at the start of their shift, express the company spirit, or 'shafu' and encourage gratitude and loyalty. Although this is usually associated with Japanese and Korean companies, IBM first published their own song book in 1927! KPMG, PwC and McKinsey & Co have all had their own Company Songs.

The energy boosting effect comes from maintaining a rhythm and singing out loud. One song for just three minutes will give a boost of adrenaline to invigorate you.

Singing requires breath control. Hammering out a full song means plenty of extra oxygen pumping around your blood vessels, not to mention the adrenaline of hitting the crescendo.

One study showed singing significantly increased energy levels among college students – noticeably more than just listening quietly. Strewth, who could have guessed that?

If you feel up to it at work and have an OK voice, a

quick one-song rock out loud session can be a great way to get invigorated. If you are in a large office, some people may be happy to sing along. Make sure you choose a song that everyone can sing along with, though, and of course make it clear they should only join in if they really want to.

For a sure-fire long-term winner, join a choir.

Belly Laugh

"Laughter is an instant vacation."
Milton Berle

If you thought smiling was good, you'll find laughing multiplies the benefits! A belly laugh soon turns any mood into an exuberant one. Even if you have to force it a little at first, a big, deep guffaw is incredible.

Try it.

- Start with belting out a ho-ho-ho and a hee-hee-hee and take it from there for a minute or so.
- Gradually the real laughter will take over.

Remember: change your physiology and you can change your mind.

The effort involved in a proper belly laugh — one that involves creasing your eyes — works your body so much that you produce endorphins that will make you feel on top of the world. You'll benefit from doing it alone, although the effect can be multiplied many times over if done together with other people simply because laughter is contagious and everyone gets sucked in.

Laughter reduces the level of stress hormones. It also increases the level of health-enhancing hormones such as endorphins.

A decent laugh sets your body tingling and you can physically feel the energy rising like a sap. A pleasant further side effect is that laughing temporarily raises your pain threshold.

Laughter yoga is a movement that started in India and is rapidly spreading all over the world. It is being increasingly used in business environments to improve the energy and performance in teams.

Pretty cool. Who said professionals can't have fun?

Power Breathe In And Out

> "Learning how to inhale completely and how to exhale completely is one of the best energisers"
> Dr. Laurel Clark, School of Metaphysics, Missouri.

Take two minutes to breathe yourself into a more energised and focused state. Breathing from the diaphragm gets energy flowing.

For the main part, controlled breathing is highly recommended as a calming, tension-busting activity, so is also mentioned in Chapter 1. Performed differently, it can be a powerful energy booster.

Olympic athletes don't breathe deeply just to get calm – they also do it to focus their energies ready for an explosive release. Watch how a weightlifter prepares to hoist a ridiculously huge load above his head, or how the cliff divers of Acapulco focus their attentions before launching into mid-air.

- Sit with your spine straight, eyes closed. Focus all of your attention on your breathing
- Put your hands on your lower ribs and feel your chest expand into your hands
- Slowly inhale to a count of six. Hold your breath to a count of three and tense the muscles in your body
- Exhale for a count of eight, completely releasing all of the breath, relaxing the muscles as you do so
- Finally, hold the breath out to a count of three.

Repeat this rhythmic count – inhale, hold and tense your body, exhale and relax, hold the breath out. Keep it to 4-6 times or you may end up feeling a bit light headed.

Breathing in stimulates your stress 'fight-or-flight' system and breathing out stimulates your 'rest-and-digest', healing system.

Yawn

Yawning is the body's way to cool down the brain, which effectively wakes it up, according to research reported in 'Psychology & Behavior', May 2014.

The researchers from the University of Vienna, the SUNY College at Oneonta USA and Nova South Eastern University in Fort Lauderdale USA concluded that cooling the brain works to improve arousal and mental efficiency.

> *"As yawning cools the brain, it gets the brain in optimal homeostasis, which is of course nice when you want to be alert, for example in a threatening situation"*
> Jorg Massen, University of Vienna.

The team also noted that previous research has not produced a link between yawning and blood oxygen levels, putting into doubt the popular idea that yawning increases the oxygen supply to the brain.

So when you feel you need more energy – yawn.

Change Your Socks

This is so simple it's amazing.

If you wear socks regularly, take a fresh pair with you and change them during the day. You'll be amazed at how much fresher you'll feel. This is especially handy on days where there may be a lot of walking or standing around involved such as during a hike or family outing. It also works an absolute treat in a business environment.

Use it to generate a bit of extra zip to prepare for the post lunch 'graveyard shift' in office and training environments when energy levels are low.

Walk Barefoot

In direct contrast to 'Change Your Socks', taking your shoes and socks off and walking around barefoot can have dramatic effects too.

The soles of the feet have a high concentration of nerve endings which makes them especially sensitive. That means that your brain receives an intense amount of input whenever you walk barefoot.

Maybe it's the contrast to your feet being cooped up inside your shoes. Maybe it's because it is just different from 'the norm'. Or maybe it is the direct contact with the shape, texture and feel of the surface, barefoot feels good. It's even better if you walk on soil, grass or sand.

Going barefoot can give all sorts of longer term benefits such as improving balance and posture and restoring your natural stride, which strengthens leg muscles that may have fallen into disuse over time.

For now, though, walking barefoot can give you an immediate buzz of energy.

Walk In Nature

A ten minute walk in the fresh air provides enough energy to feel alive for two hours. It is even more effective if you walk in nature. A local park or garden would do if you haven't got any 'nature' nearby.

Research from North Western University, Chicago found that morning light helps synchronise your body clock to regulate metabolism. They found that morning walkers sleep better, are more energised and are thinner. They also found that a 20-30 minute morning walk is the best time of day and provides the greatest energy boost of all. If you're not up for an early stroll, any daylight before noon provides almost as big a boost.

Walking in natural light raises your endorphin levels and subtly generates more energy. As you will see later, it also helps you to calm down stressful feelings.

Combine your walk with 'being in the moment'. Look for a picture in a cloud, watch a bird, really look at water flowing, watch a fire, look at trees, hear the sounds around you, be aware of the temperature of the air. Notice and drink in every detail. Walk barefoot to help, engage every one of your senses to connect in any way possible.

Good News, Bad News

There is a positive angle to everything.

"No there isn't" said caring reviewer. "What about tragedies, murder or sudden death?" To which I say "Yes, everything" although you sometimes need to look quite hard for it.

Also known as the 'Positivity Game', 'Good news, bad news' encourages a positive nature and generates energy and enthusiasm by the bucket load. It usually generates laughter very quickly and encourages participants to think flexibly by considering the situation from many different angles to squeeze out a response.

- The game involves one person starting off with some good news
- The second person has to quickly follow with a "The bad news is..."
- If there are more people in the conversation, they should then add more comments, alternating between 'good' and 'bad' news in turn, trying to out-do each other with outrageous claims.

Anybody familiar with the brilliant BBC radio programme '*I'm Sorry, I Haven't a Clue*' or the spectacularly funny American TV show '*Whose Line is it Anyway?*' may recognise it.

This can be used as a workshop opener as it quickly gets everybody involved early, encourages lateral thinking and a positive mindset and, of course, invariably ends up in ice-breaking laughter.

The energy and enthusiasm generated in a short period of time is remarkable, although you do usually need someone else to bounce off.

This game is an example of making connections, flexibility and positivity in practice. These are, of course, key fuels for your reboot.

Stand Up And Leave Your Desk

A study in early 2014 suggested that to work at an optimal level it is best to take a break of 17 minutes every 52 minutes to allow your brain to rejuvenate.

Getting away from your work at regular intervals helps re-energise and refocus. Whether it's a quick walk or a longer lunch, take time away.

Sitting for prolonged periods is really bad for your health too. It is becoming a major silent danger in our society. Sitting for long periods of time badly affects posture, flexibility, circulation and the strength of your core muscles. And it makes overeating even more likely. Indeed, even if you increase exercise for an hour a day it doesn't override the negative effects of sitting for eight hours at a stretch.

Standing up and walking around refreshes your mind and body, gets your circulation going and provides natural energy. After all you'd do it on a plane journey so it makes sense to do it in your everyday life.

Getting away from your desk may solve that problem you've been mulling over all morning too. Taking the focus away from a problem often allows the solution to materialise from your subconscious.

Taking regular breaks has benefits all round.

Set The Temperature

Rooms at optimum temperature (77°F / 25° C) makes for a happier working environment and psychologically people typically associate warmth with trust. That makes you feel good in your surroundings and so your confidence and energy rises.

Being too cold can cause the body's temperature to drop, which tells it that it's time to sleep. A study at Cornell University found that when temperatures are low in an office (68° F / 20° C), employees became more distracted and made 44% more mistakes than at the optimal temperature.

Other research findings by the Girls Day School Trust in the UK has found that girls do better in warmer classrooms (75° F/ 24° C) and boys learn better in colder rooms (70° F / 21° C).

Of course, being too warm causes drowsiness and discomfort so getting it right makes a big difference to your energy levels. Optimum temperature equals optimum performance.

Stand Strong

First mentioned in Step 1, standing tall gives you an immediate energy and confidence boost.

- Stand as if there is a thread attached to the top of your head pulling you gently upwards
- Allow this to gently, naturally elongate your neck and spine
- Then tuck in your chin, slide your shoulder blades into your back pocket and brace your stomach
- Now breathe in nice and deeply
- As you breathe out, cry "Nnnyyyyyyaaaaahhhhhh..."

All of these small movements add up to make you feel taller, more poised both mentally and physically, and more confident. Your brain releases feel-good chemicals and you quickly start to feel a lot better.

The very act of standing tall uses many muscles to support you, your head tilts upwards and you will find that a smile appears very easily.

Change your physiology, change your mind.

Sniff A Bit Of Citrus Or Herb

Sniff citrus fruits for an immediate energy boost. Citrus scents like orange, lemon and lime, stimulate alertness.

Some research has shown that when people at nightclubs are exposed to orange (or, indeed peppermint) scents, they report more positive experiences and go on to dance the night away.

To create a bit of instant energy, rub some essential oils with citrus odours or even the smell of cinnamon onto your wrists.

Other research has shown that the scent of lavender can actually increase speed and accuracy when performing mathematical computations despite the participants feeling drowsier. It also lifts mood.

In this example, students were given a mathematics test before and after being treated to three minutes of lavender aromatherapy. The group completed the tests faster and more accurately after the lavender aromatherapy. A second group were treated with rosemary oil. They were also faster but not more accurate at completing the calculations.

Yet another study showed that smelling lemon actually improved subjects' moods as well as generating more energy.

Have Sex

When you search for things to give you more energy, this advice pops up just about everywhere. It is advised equally frequently for men and for women, and works for all (legal) ages.

Sex is one great endorphin rush. Keep those endorphins flowing regularly and you will have more natural energy. Literally, more bounce to your step.

Sit Up Straight

Sit up straight to get more energy. It's in the posture.

Sit straight and you'll look and feel better too. Slouching restricts the space your vital organs have to function in, so maintaining your posture will enable them to work more efficiently. Allowing more oxygen flow helps you to feel more energised. It will even boost your self-confidence.

So ease your shoulders back, keep your chin lightly tucked in, focus your eyes dead ahead and keep your lower back slightly arched.

Take A Short Power Nap

Revitalise and recover with a short power nap.

The siesta — the word originates from the Latin phrase 'hora sexta', which means the sixth hour and counting six hours on from dawn brings about the midday rest —.is a well-established part of life in many parts of the world for one very good reason – it works.

Recline in your seat if you can. If you lie down on the sofa you could find it difficult to get back up. Keep it to about 10-20 minutes maximum. Much longer and you will drift into the deep part of your sleep cycle and it could have the opposite effect of knocking you out for the rest of the day.

An interesting extension to this idea is to drink a cup of coffee just before you nap. Caffeine takes 20 minutes to kick in so when you wake you will be buzzing.

My own favourite place to nap is in the car. A twenty minute snooze when tired from driving is invigorating and always manages to surprise me at how refreshing it is. I go out like a light then wake up quickly and easily.

Try A Bit Of Acupressure

Massaging specific points on your body is a quick way to boost energy flow. These short acupressure techniques are fast, effective and easy to do.

Use any of these variations:
- Rub your scalp or temples with your fingertips in a gentle circular motion
- Rub each earlobe between your thumb and forefinger
- Place your forefingers behind your ears where the base of your skull meets the top of your neck and press for ten seconds.
- Gently pinch the point between your thumb and forefinger for a minute for a quick energy boost

A deep massage of your shoulder muscles will have a similarly quick effect to pick you up.

(On this point we did get a nice note from a highly precise reviewer: "Technically that's not acupressure". I know. But it fits in here.)

"Massage stimulates your nerve endings, which increases blood flow and gets your circulation pumping"
Maureen Moon, former president, American Massage Therapy Association.

Perform A Random Act Of Kindness

This is the gift that keeps on giving. Just as you get energy from other peoples' attitude, so you can get charged up through other peoples' happiness and naturally expressed gratitude.

A fundamental aspect of human behaviour is the need to get on with people. We are social animals. By helping we are extending a welcoming and supportive hand.

Making other people feel good takes you away from selfish, self-centred thoughts and leaves you with a glowing sensation of goodness inside. It can improve your self-esteem when you put a small bit of effort into making your little part of the world a tiny bit kinder. Research has consistently shown that helping people makes you feel better.

It's not rocket science, it's instinctive common sense. Isn't it?

So, do something out of the blue to help somebody – ideally unexpected. Then get out of the way – don't hang around for thanks. The act of kindness is for them, not you. You will get your energising rewards from the feel-good sensation and the knowledge of making somebody else happy.

A secret millionaire in America famously used to leave envelopes containing $60 so that people could treat themselves to something pleasant when they found them.

A generous woman in Ohio found a forgotten $20 note in her purse, so used it to pay the road tolls for the cars behind her. Some were full of families and they all made a point of catching her up and waving their thanks. A special moment had been made for the giver and the receivers.

A YouTube video that went viral tells the heart-warming story of 'The Man in the Queue' who pays for a treat for a family who can't afford it because someone had done exactly that for him when he was a child. Words are unnecessary to appreciate the impact of such generosity of spirit. It's a beautiful video, too.

There is actually a non-profit making foundation for Random Acts of Kindness! The Random Acts of Kindness Week (RAK Week) is usually held in the second week of February and the World Kindness Day is in November each year.

Suck A Lemon

Citrus flavours activate nerves in the mouth, throat and nose that trigger the brain into action according to David Labbe, Ph.D., a sensory scientist at the Nestle Research Center in Switzerland.

Try it – it gives you a zest for life.

And finally, the most powerful and effective technique of them all...

Talk To People

Be friendly. Talk and listen. Shoot the breeze. Have a chuckle. Share your thoughts.

The importance of communication has been a constant thread throughout this book and talking deserves to be treated as a tool in itself. Active, two-way conversation stimulates the brain and reduces misunderstanding. It introduces humour, friendship, enjoyment, sharing and sociability, indeed it enhances all of the special characteristics that make us human.

Talking to people brings about new ideas, new perspectives and experiences. It has an uncanny ability to open doors and create opportunities where previously there were none. Yet it is so easy to forget to talk when you are busy.

As a professional by our definition you will probably already know this although, as with so many things, the knowledge may have become submerged in the general busy-ness of life.

Talking –the greatest and most effective tool of all.

Points to Ponder 4

- Talk Loudly
- 'Do' – Even If It Is Just One Thing
- Write Down Your Good Points
- Look Fabulous
- Smile
- Eat Chocolate
- Mirror And Pace
- Splash Water On Your Face
- Stand Up And Smile While You Dial
- Have A Short Burst Of Activity
- Play Loud Music
- Howl At The Moon
- Take A Hot Bath, Shower Or Sauna
- Sing
- Belly Laugh
- Power Breathe In And Out

Having a set of quick acting actions to hand can help you to raise your RAH! quotient whenever you need.

These 32 tools are entirely under your control and even a relatively small action can have a major impact on how you and others feel.

- Yawn
- Change Your Socks
- Walk Barefoot
- Walk In Nature
- Good News, Bad News
- Stand Up And Leave Your Desk
- Set The Temperature
- Stand Strong
- Sniff A Bit Of Citrus Or Herb
- Have Sex
- Sit Up Straight
- Take A Short Power Nap For 10-20 Minutes
- Try A Bit Of Acupressure
- Perform A Random Act Of Kindness
- Suck A Lemon
- Talk To People.

Try them all. Every one is worth it.

Epilogue

> *"Life is a circle. The end of one journey
> is the beginning of the next"*
> Joseph M. Marshall III

When you started on this reboot programme, you needed it. Chances are that you were slowing down, feeling more than a bit deflated and fed up. Maybe even burned out. At the very least you were a Worn Out Professional and were looking for a quick and relatively easy way out, to move from Down to Up.

This book was designed to provide that. I hope it has met those targets. The first two steps suggested that you consider your fundamental drivers; the third step provided a toolkit of the finest, proven methods to generate enthusiasm and energy that you could use in isolation or together as it suits you and your personal and professional circumstances.

Your reboot need cost nothing other than the price of the book. If you applied even some of the tips you should have more time, look better and feel happier. Fresh energy is coursing through your system and you have the tools to turn it up or down as you need.

You are facing forwards with your head up and should now be starting to feel as if you are back in control. Which puts you at an exciting junction. You have plenty of knowledge and experience and the whole of the rest of your life ahead of you.

To paraphrase Walt Disney –

'You have a lot of story yet to tell.'

Please Leave A Review

If you enjoyed reading this book, please post a review on the site where you bought it. And of course, please feel free to spread the word and encourage your friends to read it too!

Next up — my thanks go to...

Acknowledgements

For Betsan, my beautiful wife since 1982 and our four wonderful children.

Thanks for your patience and encouragement.

You thrill and inspire me each day with your continued development and growth.

Reading Group Discussion

Sometimes in a Reading Group it can be difficult to know where to start conversation about a book, so here are a few suggestions:

- With the current levels of burnout in so many professions, do you think this book is relevant and timely?
- What is your eulogy?
- Can you state your eulogy in less than 25 words?
- What is your story?
- What are the five most significant decision points in your life?
- How could the Worn Out Professional's partner help them to engage in these tips?
- Have you ever done anything similar to a reboot?
- Do you know of anyone this book could help?
- Can you relate to this personally?

I hope you have some interesting discussions and would love to hear about them. Contact details are on the final page of this book.

About the Author

Steve Corkhill is a successful independent change management consultant, coach and entrepreneur and in 2014 began his journey into writing and self-publishing. His mission in life is to help worn out professionals regain their enthusiasm, energy and drive so they can enjoy performing at their best once again.

The decision to write this book became obvious when he and colleagues recognised that they had been glaring examples of Worn Out Professionals a good few times over the years. So the research was put together.

Steve considers himself to be lucky. He is honestly able to say that he has always loved his work for 90% of the time and reckons that the other 10% needs to happen to make the rest of it as enjoyable as it is. Or to give a nudge that it's time to move on. It's a statistics thing.

Also by Steve Corkhill

How To Recover From Open Heart Surgery

Once he was past the initial shock of being told that he needed open heart surgery, Ben's thoughts turned to practical matters. No work meant no income for him and his family, so he really needed answers to three simple questions:

What should he expect?

What could he do to speed up a recovery?

And how long was he likely to be out of action for?

Based on true events, the story traces an absorbing series of misguided expectations, camaraderie and a rollercoaster ride of highs and lows as Ben tried to meet his own definition of 'recovery'. It reflects what Ben felt as he experienced a series of what felt like miraculous medical events designed to fix his condition.

Written for the hundreds of thousands of people who will find themselves in a similar position this year.

Comments from reviewers:
> *"This will be immensely reassuring to anyone going through this experience."*
> *"Enthralling.' I didn't want to put it down. Everyone knows somebody who has had similar fears."*
> *"Hugely encouraging and enlightening."*
> *"Great to highlight this, so other families will know what to expect."*

This is a practical example of "Reboot For The Worn Out Professional" in practice. Every single technique outlined was used by Ben in his quest for 'recovery'.

More by Steve Corkhill

Under the pen-name of 'Barney Hegarty', the Laugh Out Loud emails series, made up of:

The Art Of Miscommunication – Announcers and Help Desks
The Art Of Miscommunication – Letters, Forms and Replies
The Art Of Miscommunication – Comebacks and Answers

Battle Of The Sexes – The Joy Of Marriage
Battle Of The Sexes – War Of The Worlds
Battle Of The Sexes – Men On Mars And Venus
Battle Of The Sexes – Women On Venus And Mars
Battle Of The Sexes – Stereotypes

Tales Of The Unexpected – True And Embarrassing
Tales Of The Unexpected – Did I Know That?

Connect with Steve

To connect with Steve use:
Twitter: https://twitter.com/SteveCorkhill
Facebook: https://www.facebook.com/steve.ftwop
Email: Steve.Corkhill@FTWOP.com

www.ingramcontent.com/pod-product-compliance
Lightning Source LLC
Chambersburg PA
CBHW061326040426
42444CB00011B/2789